Handbook of Latin Inscriptions

Illustrating The History Of The Language

W. M. Lindsay

Alpha Editions

This Edition Published in 2020

ISBN: 9789354213397

Design and Setting By
Alpha Editions
www.alphaedis.com
Email – info@alphaedis.com

As per information held with us this book is in Public Domain. This book is a reproduction of an important historical work. Alpha Editions uses the best technology to reproduce historical work in the same manner it was first published to preserve its original nature. Any marks or number seen are left intentionally to preserve its true form.

PREFACE.

WHILE writing my *Short Historical Latin Grammar*, I often wished that there was a suitable collection of specimens of Latin, chronologically arranged, to which the student might be referred. The proposal of Messrs. Allyn and Bacon, that a Handbook of Latin Inscriptions illustrative of the history of the language should be compiled for their educational series, was therefore very welcome. From merely turning over the pages of a book of this kind one will sometimes learn more than from the most elaborate array of rules, just as the successive pictures of a panorama are often more instructive than the showman's lecture.

In a few cases, where it seemed advisable, documents which cannot strictly be called 'Inscriptions' have been included (Nos. 4, 65, 67, 78, 83, 84). The expression of long *i* by *i* with an apex, instead of by the tall form of the letter, in Chap. III., is a concession to typographical convenience.

W. M. LINDSAY.

OXFORD, ENGLAND, August, 1897.

CONTENTS.

CHAP.		PAGE
I.	THE EARLIEST PERIOD AND THE BEGINNING OF LITERATURE	1
II.	THE PERIOD OF THE REPUBLICAN LITERATURE	47
III.	THE AGE OF CICERO AND THE EARLY EMPIRE. CLASSICAL LATIN	94
IV.	IMPERIAL AND LATE LATIN	114
INDEX		131

HANDBOOK

OF

LATIN INSCRIPTIONS.

CHAPTER I.

THE EARLIEST PERIOD AND THE BEGINNING OF LITERATURE.

1. Latin belongs to the same family of languages as Greek, and the farther back we can trace the Latin speech, the more we find it resembling the Greek forms and inflexions. But there was one thing which, century by century, altered more and more the appearance of Latin words, and that was the Latin accent. The Latin accent was, like ours, an accent of stress. The accented syllable was uttered so strongly as to spoil the clear utterance of the following syllables; and just as in our own language the noun 'minute,' derived from Latin *mĭnūtum*, has come to be pronounced 'minit' instead of 'minute,' so too in Latin a word like *genos* came to be pronounced indistinctly, incorrectly, irrationally, as *genus*. The cause of the change is the same in the Latin as in the English word. We use most of the breath at our disposal in uttering the first syllable of the word 'minute,'

and leave the following syllable without a chance of being properly pronounced. Precisely in the same way the Roman put the strength of his voice into the utterance of the first syllable of *genos*, with the result that the second syllable was not given its full, proper sound of -*nos*, but was hurried over in such a fashion that the sound that reached the ear was rather -*nus* than -*nos*. But there is this difference between the Latin language and our own. Though we have long since abandoned the correct pronunciation 'minūte' and have universally adopted the careless utterance 'minĭt,' we still keep the old spelling. A Roman, however, spelled as he pronounced; so that when he became conscious that the way in which he pronounced *genos* was really with the sound of *u* not of *o* in the second syllable, he gave up the old spelling *genos* and adopted a new spelling, *genus*. That is what is meant by saying that Roman spelling was phonetic, while ours is traditional.

2. Of the alterations undergone by Latin words and inflexions from one century to another, the most noticeable were the changes in unaccented vowels, such as the vowel of the second syllable of *genos*, Class. Lat. *genus*. If we remove these alterations and restore the words to their proper vocalism, the affinity of Latin with Greek is much more easy to perceive. The older form of *gĕnŭs*, namely *gĕnŏs*, is exactly identical with the corresponding Greek word γένος, if we pronounce the Latin word as the Romans pronounced it, with 'hard' *g*. Again, the Latin Second Declension looks as if it were different from the Greek; for the typical Latin ending is -*ŭs*, while the

Greek is -ος. But here, too, it is merely the Latin weakening of unaccented vowels that has effaced the resemblance. Before the Latin stress-accent on the first syllable had fully exerted its weakening influence on the second, a word like dŏlŭs was pronounced and spelled dŏlŏs, with the same ending -ŏs as Greek δόλος or any other noun of the Second Declension. Thus the farther back we go in the history of the Latin language, the more we find its forms resembling the Greek vocalism; and in studying Latin forms we must always bear in mind that the great influence at work in changing their appearance was the Latin accentuation.

3. What, then, were the rules of Latin accentuation, and at what periods in the history of Rome did it bring about these alterations in the vowels of unaccented syllables?

At some very early time, it is impossible to say precisely when, every Latin word was accented on the first syllable. The Perfect of *fallo*, for example, had the accent on the syllable *fe-*, and that is why the second syllable whose proper pronunciation was *-fall-* (with an ă) came, in time, to be pronounced and spelled *-fell-* (with an ĕ). We, with an accent of much the same type as the Roman, can easily realize how *féfalli* passed gradually into *féfelli;* for in our own pronunciation of words like 'prevalent' we see the same weakening, hurrying over, or slurring of the unaccented syllable. Similarly, the old name *Nŭmăsio-* became *Numesio-*, and in time (see § 6) *Numerio-*.

At what time it was that this practice arose of throwing the weight of the voice on the first syllable of each and every Latin word we cannot tell, nor yet at what precise period the new fashion came in of accenting the antepenultimate syllable where the penult was short and the penult itself where it was long. The new fashion is the rule of Classical Latin; e.g. *dedécŏris*, Gen. of *dedecus*, is accented on the antepaenultima because the paenultima is a short syllable, while *decŏ́ris*, Gen. of *decor*, having a long penult, is accented on the penult. We may guess that the change — a gradual, not a sudden, one — took place about 350–250 B.C., and that words like *Nŭmĕ̆rius*, that is to say, words of four syllables with the first three short, were still later in succumbing to the new tendency. The accent probably persisted on the first syllable of such words (cf. our 'căpĭtălist') till the beginning of the first century B.C. But we know that the 'Older Law of Accentuation,' as it is called, was long enough in practice to leave its mark, where possible, on the second syllable of each and every word of the language. It is the syllable immediately following the accented syllable which in a language with stress-accentuation is always the chief sufferer. The old Latin accent being, as we have seen, on the first syllable of each word, it was the second syllable of the word which lay most exposed to its masterful influence. The only kind of second syllables which resisted that influence successfully were syllables which had a long simple vowel. *Decēdo*, for example, preserved its second syllable unimpaired, but *de-caido* became *deceido*, then *decīdo;* and *de-cădo* became *decĕdo*, then *decĭdo*. Sometimes the short vowel was driven out of its place altogether; *re-pĕperi* became *repperi*, and *re-tĕtuli, rettuli*.

The effect of this 'Old Law of Accentuation' on the language was enormous. Every word which had a short second syllable had that syllable effaced by Syncope or else altered by Vowel-weakening, an ă becoming an ĕ (later ĭ, see below). Every word which had a diphthong in the second syllable had that diphthong altered; *ai* to *ei* (later written and pronounced ī), *au* (through *eu*?) to *ou* (later written and pronounced ū).

4. The adoption of the new law of accentuation, the 'Paenultima Law,' as it is called, did not arrest the process of Vowel-weakening. In the course of the third century B.C. we see ĕ reduced to ĭ; *concĕdo* (earlier *concado*) becomes *concĭdo*; *aget*, 3d Sg. Pres. Ind., becomes *agĭt*. Ŏ, when unaccented, sinks to ŭ; *genŏs* becomes *genus*. The precise rules of Vowel-weakening and Syncope cannot be given here. They may be learned from historical grammars such as my *Historical Latin Grammar*, ch. ii. §§ 12 sqq., Bennett, *Appendix*, §§ 71 sqq.

5. In the first part of the period illustrated in this section, we must think of the language as dominated by the 'Older Law of Accentuation,' with an accent of stress on all first syllables, an accent which gradually weakened or effaced the vowel of the second syllable. And not merely the second syllable, but the final syllable too suffered under the overpowering influence of the stress-accentuation of the beginning of the word. *Ai* in a final syllable became in time *ei* (Class. Lat. ī), and *oi* suffered the same change. Thus the ī of the Nom. Plur. of the

Second Declension, which was pronounced *ei* up to about 150 B.C. and was written *ei* even later, was originally *oi*. The Dat. Abl. Plur. of the same Declension ended originally in *-ois*, which passed by the usual Vowel-weakening to *-eis*, Class. Lat. *-īs*. The *-ai* of the Dat. Sg. of the Third Declension became *-ei*, Class. Lat. *-i*, and so on. Our oldest inscription (No. 1) belongs to a time when this Vowel-weakening had not so far developed as to be recognized in the spelling: thus we have *Număsio-*, not *Numĕsio-*; *fefăked*, not *feféked*.

6. We cannot assign a date to the earliest examples of Vowel-weakening. But another phonetic change, which effected almost as great an alteration in the appearance of Latin words, we can date with some probability. Between vowels an *s* became *r* in Latin, a process called 'Rhotacism,' in the course of the fourth century B.C., just as in Greek an *s* in the same position became at first *h*, then was dropped. If we eliminate these changes from the Latin and Greek case-forms of a word like *genos*, γένος, we see how similar is the early declension in the two languages: —

Singular:

Nom. *gĕnŏs* (γένος)   which became *genus* (γένος),
Gen. (1) *gĕnĕsĕs*   "   "   *generis*,
 (2) *gĕnĕsŏs* (γένεσος) "   "   *generus*, an occasional form
           (γένεος, then γένους),
Dat. *gĕnĕsai*   "   "   *generei* (Class. Lat. *generī*),
Loc. *gĕnĕsĭ* (γένεσι)   "   "   *genere* (γένεϊ, then γένει),
           in Latin with Ablative
           use, in Greek with Dative.

The Earliest Period.

Plural:

Nom. *gĕnĕsa* (γένεσα)   which became *genera* (γένεα, then γένη),
Gen. *gĕnĕsōm* (γενέσων)   "   "   *generŏm*, then *generŭm*
(γενέων, then γενῶν),

and so on.

Our two oldest Latin inscriptions (Nos. 1 and 2) belong to a time when this change of intervocalic *s* to *r* had not yet been effected. Thus we have *Numasio-* for Class. Lat. *Numerio-*, *Toitesia-* not *-eria-*.

7. Another characteristic of this early period is that the diphthongs still remained intact. For the Latin diphthongs, even when in the accented syllable, came in course of time to have their true pronunciation modified. The true, original pronunciation gave the diphthong the combined sound of its separate elements. *Oi* was pronounced with the sound of *o* immediately followed by the sound of *i*; *ai* with the sound of *a* immediately followed by the sound of *i*. But in time the neighbourhood of *i* affected the *o*, and the *o* came to be pronounced like German ö; then the *i* sunk to *e*, and this öe, written *oe*, came finally to be uttered as if it were the simple vowel *ū*. The root of the word *Toitesia-* is apparently the same word with which we are familiar in Classical Latin under the form *tūtus*. Similarly the *a* of *ai* became ä under the influence of the neighbouring *i*; then the *i* sunk to *e*, and what was originally *ai* came to be pronounced äe and written *ae*; while the last stage of all, the descent into the simple vowel-sound *e*, was reserved for the Post-classical period.

This, then, constitutes an unfamiliar feature of the

older language, the retention of the diphthongs in their original form, *ai*, *oi*, *ou*, and so on. Cf. my *Historical Grammar*, ch. x. § 11, Bennett, *App.*, §§ 80 sqq.

8. With the forms of the letters in which the language was written at this early epoch we need not much concern ourselves, for the object of our study is the history of the language itself, and not the history of its writing. But it may be mentioned that the Romans took their alphabet bodily from the Greek colonists who were their neighbours, and adopted the habit of writing in the first instance for the purpose of trading with them. The early Latin alphabet is thus nothing but the Greek alphabet; and though on Greek soil these early forms of letters developed in one direction and on Latin soil in another, the Greek and Latin alphabets with which we are familiar still shew enough resemblance to convince us of their original identity. The Romans retained Q, the Greek Koppa, a letter which went out of use in the Attic alphabet, but they dropped letters like Theta and Phi, which had no sounds in the Latin pronunciation to correspond to them. To express the peculiarly Roman sound *f* they used at first the Greek combination of the Digamma, the sign of our sound of *w*, with the sign for our sound of *h*. These two signs in the old Greek alphabet were F and H, and the combination FH expressed a sound occasionally found in early Greek words which came near the early Roman sound of *f*. Thus in our earliest Latin inscription the ancient Perfect (3d Sg.) of *facio*, viz. *fĕfăkeid* is written FHEFHAKED, with the *f*-sound expressed by the double sign FH. The incon-

venience of having a double symbol for a single sound led to the dropping of the second element, so that F became the Latin letter to express the sound *f*. The E in the last syllable of FHEFHAKED probably expresses the sound of the diphthong *ei*, for in the early Greek alphabet the letter E stood for what would in the Attic Greek of Demosthenes' time be written (1) ε, (2) η, (3) ει.

The K of FHEFHAKED is another feature of early Latin writing. The Greek Kappa expressed the sound in Greek that corresponded to the Latin 'unvoiced' guttural, and was at first always used in this function. But the Greeks pronounced their *k*-sound in a way that seemed to a Roman ear as much like a *g*-sound as a *k*-sound; and so a Greek word like κυβερνῶ was written by the Romans in their own characters with a *g*, *guberno*. The result of this want of clear distinction between the *k*- and the *g*-sound in Greek pronunciation was that the Romans used the letter Gamma, written C or < in the early Greek alphabet, as often for a *k*-sound as for a *g*-sound, and in course of time came to drop almost entirely the symbol K, using C to express both the *k*-sound and the *g*-sound. When at last the necessity for distinguishing these sounds forced itself upon them, instead of reverting to the old usage of K for the *k*-sound and C for the *g*-sound, they invented a new symbol for the *g*-sound by adding a stroke to the C. That is the origin of the Roman letter G. See my *Historical Grammar*, ch. i. § 5, Bennett, *App.*, §§ 1, 3.

In the Dvenos Inscription (No. 2) the *g*-sound of *virgo* and the *k*-sound of *cosmis* are written with the same letter C or <, while the *k*-sound of *pakari* is expressed by K; so that this inscription gives us a good example of the early indiscriminate use of these letters. We must not, however, suppose that *virgo* was pronounced with the *c*- or *k*-sound. Though written -CO it was pronounced -GO, just as the names *Gāius* and *Gnaeus* in Classical Latin were in abbreviations written in the old-fashioned style *C.*, *Cn.*, though they were never pronounced with any but the *g*-sound.

9. Of the forms of Declension and Conjugation which may have prevailed in this earliest period, we can say little. It is a common case in the history of a language, that its early stages are marked by an abundance of forms of which, in later stages, only 'the fittest' survive. How many and how various modes of declining Nouns and Pronouns and of conjugating Verbs may have sunk in the 'struggle for existence' before we have sufficient records of the language, we cannot tell. Our earliest inscription shews us a Perfect of *facio* whose existence we should never have guessed, had it not been thus accidentally preserved to us. *Fĕfăkei* was an old by-form of *fĕkei* (Class. Lat. *fēcī*), as *pĕpĭgi* is of *pēgi*. But how many similar by-forms the Perfects of other Verbs may have had, it is impossible to say. It is a significant fact that our second oldest inscription, the Dvenos Inscription, though nearly every letter of it can be determined with exactness, is yet in great part unintelligible to us. We cannot with certainty assign to some of its forms equivalents in Classical Latin.

10. But from the middle of the third century B.C. we have more material for ascertaining the actual forms

The Earliest Period.

of the early language, and can draw up paradigms of the Declensions in some such shape as this:—

First Declension, e.g. *terra*.

SING.

Nom. *terrā*, then *terră*

Gen. (1) *terrās* (cf. class. *paterfamilias*)
(2) *terrāī*, then *terrāi*

Dat. *terrāi*, which became (1) *terrā*, afterwards dropped, (2) *terrai*

Acc. *terrăm*, then *terrăm*

Abl. *terrād*

PLUR.

Nom. *terrāi*, then *terrai*

Gen. *terrāsŏm*, then *terrārŏm*

Dat. Abl. *terrais*, then *terreis*

Acc. *terrās*

Second Declension, e.g. *dŏlŏs* (class. *dŏlŭs*).

SING.

Nom. M. *dolŏs*
(N. *donŏm*)

Gen. *dolī*

Dat. *dolōi*, which became (1) *dolō*, (2) *dolōi*, afterwards dropped

Acc. *dolŏm*

Voc. *dolĕ*

Abl. *dolōd*

PLUR.

Nom. M. *doloi*, then *dolei*
(N. *donā*, then *donă*)

Gen. (1) *dolōm*, then *dolŏm*
(2) *dolōsŏm*, then *dolōrŏm*

Dat. Abl. *dolois*, then *doleis*

Acc. *dolōs*

Third Declension, e.g. *gĕnŏs* (class. *gĕnŭs*).

SING.

Nom. N. *genŏs*

M.F. (*matĕr, oratōr, navĭs*)

Gen. (1) *genesĕs*, then *generĕs*
(2) *genesŏs*, then *generŏs*, afterwards dropped

PLUR.

Nom. N. *genesā*, then *generā*, *generă*

M.F. (*matrĕs* (?), *navēs*)

Gen. *genesŏm*, then *generŏm*

Handbook of Latin Inscriptions.

	SING.		PLUR.
Dat.	genesaí, then generei	Dat. Abl.	genesibŏs, then generĭbŏs.
Acc.	(matrĕm, navĭm)	Acc.	(matrēs, navīs)
Abl.	(1) genesĭ, then generĭ		
	(2) genesīd, then generīd		

Demonstrative Pronouns:—

    hŏ-, hĕ-, 'this'   ŏl-sŏ-, 'that'
      SING.

Nom.	M. hĕ-ce	(1) ollŏs, (2) ollŏ, then ollĕ
	F. hăi-ce	ollă, then ollă
	M. hŏd-ce, hocce	ollŏd
Gen.	hoiŏs (?)	olloiŏs, then olleiŏs
Dat.	hoi-ce (?)	olloi, then ollei
Loc.	hei-ce (the class.	ollei (cf. illī Plaut. = class.
	Adv. hīc 'here')	illīc 'there')
Acc.	M. hŏn-ce	ollŏm
	F. hăn-ce	ollăm, then -ăm
Abl.	M.N. hŏd-ce, hocce	ollŏd
	F. hăd-ce, hacce	ollăd

      PLUR.

Nom.	M. hoi, then hei (unaccented)	olloi, then ollei
	F. hăi, with Particle hăi-ce	ollăi, with Particle ollăi-ce
	N. hăi-ce	(1) ollă, (2) ollăi-ce
Gen.	M.N. hŏsŏm, then horŏm	ollŏsŏm, then ollorŏm
	F. hăsŏm, then harŏm	ollăsŏm, then ollarŏm
Dat. }	hois } then heis (un-	ollois } then olleis
Abl. }	hais } accented)	ollais }
Acc.	M. hŏs	ollŏs
	F. hăs	ollăs

The older language allowed the Particle -ce to be added or left out at will, e.g. O. Lat. haec, hae Fem. Pl.

The Earliest Period.

Relative, Indefinite (Interrogative) Pronoun:—

		quŏ-	quĭ-
		SING.	
Nom.	M.	quŏ-ĭ, then quei (unaccented)	quĭ-s
	F.	quā-ĭ	
	N.	quŏ-d	quĭ-d
Gen.		quŏ-eios, then quoios	
Dat.		quŏ-eiei, then quoiei	
Acc.	M.		quĕm
	F.	quām, then quăm	
Abl.	M.N.	quōd }	quĭd
	F.	quād }	
		PLUR.	
Nom.	M.	quoi, then quei (unaccented)	quēs
	F.	quāi	
	N.	quāi	
Gen.	M.N.	quōsōm, then quorŏm	
	F.	quāsōm, then quarŏm	
Dat. } Abl. }		quois, then queis (unaccented)	quĭbus
Acc.	M.	quōs }	quēs
	F.	quās }	

11. For the Verb we may construct a paradigm like this:—

PRES. IND. ACTIVE.		PRES. IND. PASSIVE.	
1st Sg.	legō	1st Sg.	legōr
2d Sg.	legĕs(ĭ)	2d Sg.	(1) legesŏ (?), then legesĕ, legerĕ
			(2) legerĕs
3d Sg.	legĕt(ĭ)	3d Sg.	legĕtŏr
1st Pl.	legĕmŏs	1st Pl.	legĕmŏr
2d Pl.	legĕtĕs	2d Pl.	legĕmĕnoi, then -ei
3d Pl.	legŏnt(ĭ)	3d Pl.	legŏntŏr

12. At the time when the imitation of Greek literature was begun by Livius Andronicus, c. 250 B.C., the older law of accentuation, by which the first syllable of every word received the accent (§ 3), had been replaced by the new law, the law which remained in force in classical Latin. By the new law the accent fell on the paenultima, if the paenultima were long, and on the antepaenultima if the paenultima were short. The older accentuation, however, as we have seen, still persisted in four-syllabled words of the scansion ◡ ◡ ◡ ⌣̄, e.g. *fácilius, bálineum* (class. *balneum*), *vígilia*, which did not become *facílius, vigília*, etc., till the first century B.C. It is easy to see how the change from the old to the new Accentuation Law would gradually be effected. Long words like *tempestatibus* would at all times have two accents, a main accent and a secondary, just as long words with us, e.g. 'characteristic,' have a secondary accent on the first syllable, 'char-,' as well as the main accent on the penult. Under the Old Law of Accentuation the main accent belonged to the initial syllable '*tem-*,' the secondary accent would fall on the antepenultimate syllable '*-sta-*.' Under the new law the main accent was transferred to the antepenultimate, the secondary to the initial syllable. So that the change from the old to the new accentuation in such a word as *tempestatibus* would be merely the change from *témpestàtibus* to *tèmpestátibus*.

13. In any account of the accentuation of a language this secondary accent, though it is to be found in all languages, is seldom mentioned. It is the main accent which is thought of and spoken of as 'the accent' of the word. The secondary accent of Latin words, however, seems to have played a part in that curious primitive metre which was employed by the Romans in their rude native poetry before the introduction of the artificial metres of the Greeks, and which held its place beside these foreign importations for a considerable time. It is known as the Saturnian Metre, and seems to have been, like our own metres, regulated by the accent of the word and not by the quantity (long or short) of the syllable. The Saturnian line probably consisted of two portions, the first syllable of the line being invariably accented. The first contained, as a rule, seven syllables, always with three accent-beats. The second contained, as a rule, six syllables, always with two accent-beats. The prevailing type (see *Amer. Journ. Phil.*, vol. xiv.) is:—

$$\acute{x}x(,)\quad \acute{x}x,\quad \acute{x}xx \parallel \acute{x}xx,\quad \acute{x}xx$$
dábunt málum Metélli ‖ Naévio poétae,

though another type is occasionally found:—

$$\acute{x}x(,)\quad \acute{x}x,\quad \acute{x}xx \parallel \acute{x}xxx,\quad \acute{x}x$$
prím(a) incédit Céreris ‖ Prosérpina púer.

The secondary accent is recognized in this metre in this way. Of the three accents in the first half of the line and of the two accent-beats in the second half, any one may be a secondary accent. For example, in the Scipio Epitaph, No. 25, the first half of one line is made up of the words

dédet Tèmpestátebus,

that is *dedit Tempestatibus* 'he presented to the Divinities of the Storm.' Here we have the requisite number of accent-beats in the hemistich, three in all; but they are not three main accents. There are two main accents, the accent on the first syllable of *dedet* and that on the antepaenultima of *Tempestatebus* ; but the third, the accent on the first syllable of this word, is a secondary accent.

14. The secondary accent plays a part, too, in the phonetic changes of the language, for the vowels of the syllables on which it fell were not weakened or syncopated like the unaccented vowels. The process of Vowel-weakening which began a century or more before (see § 3) continued in operation after the beginning of Roman Literature. Unaccented ŏ was weakened to ŭ, e.g. *genŭs* from older *genŏs* (cf. Gk. γένος), *dolŭs* from older *dolŏs* (cf. Gk. δόλος), a weakening which was probably fully effected in pronunciation by the end of the third century B.C., though the older spelling was often retained. Indeed, in words where an unaccented ŏ was preceded by the spirant *u* (*v*), a spirant which had the sound of our *w*, e.g. *deiuŏs*, a god, the spelling with *o* was retained down to the beginning of the Empire, through a desire to avoid the use of two *u*'s side by side, *deiuus* (*dīuus*). However, in pronunciation *deiuŏs* may very likely have become *deiuŭs* at the same time as *dolŏs* became *dolŭs*. As early as the time of Plautus we find that the last syllable has been reduced from the sound *-uus* (*-vus*) to *-us*; for it must have been from some form like *deius* that the shortened form of the word *deus* arose. Similarly *bouōm*

The Beginning of Literature.   17

(Gk. βο(ϝ)ων) Gen. Plur. of *bōs* became by the Latin Phonetic law which shortened every long vowel before a final -*m*, *bouŏm*, and this unaccented *ŏ* passed in pronunciation to *ŭ*, with the result that *bouŭm* became *boŭm*.

Unaccented *ĕ* was similarly weakened to *ĭ*. *Generis*, for example, is the new form of *generĕs*, originally *genesĕs* (§ 6). An unaccented *ă* which had before the beginning of the Roman literature sunk to *ĕ*, was accordingly now reduced a stage further to *ĭ*. But before *r* or a consonant-group the *ĕ*-sound remained. *Pepĕri* from *părio* did not become *pepĭri*, like *cecĭdi* from *cădo*. *Remĕx* from *remus* and *ăgo* did not become *remĭx*; though before a single consonant we find *ĭ* in *remĭgo*, etc.

Before a labial (*b*, *p*, *m*) the weakened vowel took the form *u*, which acquired the sound of short German ü, and in time came to be pronounced and written *ĭ*. The change to *ĭ* occurred earliest where the next syllable contained an *i* which preceded a vowel, e.g. *surrĭpio* from *răpio* (cf. *surrŭpui* in Plautus), *incĭpio* from *căpio* (cf. *occŭpo*).

15. At the same time that unaccented *ĕ* became *ĭ* and unaccented *ŏ* became *ŭ*, we find accented *ĕ* and *ŏ* in certain positions passing into the same vowel-sounds. Thus *ĕ* became *ĭ* before *ng* in words like *tĭngo* (Gk. τέγγω); *ŏ* became *ŭ* before *ng* in words like *unguis* (Gk. ὄνυξ). See *Latin Language*, ch. iv. §§ 11, 20; Bennett, *App.*, §§ 73, 76.

18   *Handbook of Latin Inscriptions.*

INSCRIPTIONS.

I. The "Praenestine fibula," a brooch [fibula] found at Praeneste (perhaps fifth cent. B.C.). (*C.I.L.* XIV. 4123.)

Manios med fefaked Numasioi.
Manius me fecit Numerio.
'Manius made me for Numerius.'

This is our oldest inscription. The vowels are not yet weakened in the syllable following the accent, which would fall at this period on the first syllable of each word (§ 3), e.g. **Númasioi**. Thus we have **fefaked**, but not yet 'fefeked'; **Numasioi**, but not yet 'Numesioi.' The first of these words, **fĕfăkēd**, is a by-form, which soon became obsolete, of the classical Perf. of *facio*, corresponding to *pĕpĭgi* beside *pēgi;* the second, **Nŭmăsioi**, is the Dative of a derivative from the root of the name *Numa*, which became in Latin *Nŭmĕrio-*, and in other dialects *Nŭmĭsio-*. Our inscription is earlier than the change of *s* between vowels to *r* (§ 6).

The style of its writing is very ancient, for the reduplication syllable **fe** is separated from the rest of the word, and the sound *f* is expressed by FH, the Greek digamma, followed by the sign for *h*. This appears to have been the earliest method of expressing the sound *f*, a sound made at this time with the two lips, not with the upper teeth and the lower lip. This bilabial *f*-sound, which may be compared to the sound we make with our lips in blowing out a candle, was, in the Greek writing of the time, expressed by this combination of

The Beginning of Literature. 19

the digamma with the letter H, a letter which was afterwards used as a symbol of the long e-sound, but whose earlier use was as a symbol of the breathing. In course of time the Romans came to drop the second half of this double symbol FH, and retained only the sign F (§ 8). On the terminations -os of **Manios**, -d of mēd, -ēd (for -eid) of **fefaked**, -oi, a diphthong, of **Numasioi**, see §§ 2, 19, 8, 10.

II. The "Dvenos bowl," a triple sacrificial bowl, found at Rome. (Egbert, *Introd. Study Lat. Inscr.*, p. 16.)

Ioueis (? -ues) at deiuos qoi med mitat nei ted endo cosmis Virco sied asted noisi Ope Toitesiai pakari uois Duenos med feced (? feked) en Manom einom dienoine med Mano statod. (Perhaps early fourth cent. B.C.)

Jovios (?) ad deos qui me mittet (? mittat), ne te indo comis Virgo sit, adstet, nisi Opem Tuteriae *pacrem vis. Benus me fecit in Manum enim. Die noni me Mano stato (i.e. *sistito*).

'Who offers me to the Gods of the Sky, may Proserpine not be kind to thee, nor stand by thee, unless thou wouldst have the Help of Tuteria propitious. Benus made me for Manus indeed. On the ninth day set me (as offering) to Manus.'

Neither the meaning nor the division into words of this inscription is certain. The rendering of it given above understands it to prescribe that the bowl is to be used only in offerings to *Manus*, one of the *Di Manes*, or gods of the lower world, but to none of the gods of the upper air. An exception is made in the case of *Ops Tuteriae*, apparently a religious designation of the same kind as the priestly invocations which Aulus Gellius (xiii. 23. 2) has preserved for us: Luam Saturni, Salaciam Neptuni, Horam Quirini, Virites Quirini, Maiam Volcani, Heriem Junonis, Moles Martis Nerienemque Martis.

Einom seems to be used like Virgil's *enim* in the line: tibi enim, tibi, maxima Juno, mactat (*A*. viii. 84).

The active use of *sto* is characteristic of Early Latin. Cf. *Jupiter Stator* 'the stayer of the rout,' *procul abstandus est* (*amor*) Plaut. *Trin.* 264, etc. The neuter sense appears in **asted**. **Duenos** would be in Class. Lat. *Bĕnus*, and is a proper name connected with the Adj. *bonus* (cf. *bene*), the old form of which was *duonus* (see my *Hist. Gram.* ch. x. § 13). **Nei**, afterwards *ni*, is used in the sense of Class. Lat. *nē*; cf. Virg. *A*. iii. 683 ni teneant cursus. **Pākări(m)** is, in the above rendering, supposed to be Acc. Sg. of a RI-stem Adj. from the root of *păx*, meaning 'propitious.' This Adj. stem *păcri-* is common in this sense in other dialects of Italy; but in Latin literature we have no example of the Adj., though the Noun *pax*, in the sense of 'divine favour,' is common enough; e.g. Plaut. *Trin.* 837 ni tua pax propitia foret praesto; Virg. *A*. x. 31, sine pace tua atque inuito numine. This use of a parasitic vowel between *c* and *r* is, however, un-Latin, and **pakari** may represent an Adj., *păcărĕm*. The formation of **noisi** is doubtful, but the sense of *nisi* is, rightly or wrongly, usually given to it. With **Nei . . . asted**, compare the Greek formula εὐιλάτου τύχοι Δήμητρος καὶ Κόρας. The word *comis* had, in later use, the more homely sense 'civil'; but cf. the oracle of Marcius (Livy, xxv. 12), ludi qui quotannis comiter Apollini fiant.

Archaic features of this inscription are: (1) the use of q for *qu* in **qoi**; (2) the distinction of the *t*-ending of the 3d Sg. Subj. **mitat** (which probably has the Fut. sense, an early sense of the Subjunctive Mood), and the *d*-ending of the 3d Sg. Opt. **sied, asted** (which here, it should be noticed, have the true Optative use, 'I pray that Proserpine may not be kind to thee, may not stand by thee'), and of the 3d Sg. Perf. Ind. **feked**; (3) the retention of the group **sm**, e.g. **cosmis**, Class. Lat. *cōmis;* (4) the use of the letter C for the *k*-sound, **cosmis**, as well as the *g*-sound, **uirco**; (5) the retention of *s* between vowels, e.g. **Toitesiai**. Whether any method is followed in the use of the guttural-symbols, **c** in **cosmis, uirco**, **k** in **pakari**, and either **c** or **k** in **feced** (? **feked**), is not easy to say (§ 8). Nor is the use of the diphthongs quite clear in **noisi, einom, noine**. Vowel-weakening appears in the post-tonic syllable of **Toitesiai** if this represent an earlier *Toitasia-* (cf. the dialectal name *Tutisulanus*), but not in the monosyllabic diphthong **qoi**.

In contrast with the Praenestine Fibula, notice **feced** for the other's **fefaked** (§ 9) and the Dat. Sg. in **-o, Mano**, for the other's **-oi, Numasioi** (§ 10).

Ioueis or **Ioues**, apparently Acc. Plur. Masc. of the IO-stem *Jovio-*, an Adj. derived from the root dyew- (Gk. Ζεύς, Lat. *Jū-piter*), the original sense of which was 'the sky.' We find mention of various *di Jovii* on inscriptions, e.g. *Venerus Joviae* (see No. 51 a), *Herculi Jovio*, etc. **at.** On this by-form of *ad*, see § 20; *Lat. Language*, chap. ii. § 76. **deiuos.** The diphthong *ei* has not yet passed into *ī* (§ 5). **qoi.** This is the older form of the diphthong. The weakened form, *ei*, which properly belonged to the unaccented use of the Relative, became in time the universal form, whence Class. Lat. *quī* (§ 5). **mēd,** see § 19. **mitat,** Class. Lat. *mittat*, probably with the sense of *mittet*. Double consonants were written with the single letter till the time of Ennius (§ 17). **nei** (see above). **ted,** old form of *tē*, as *med* of *me* (§ 19). **endo,** later *indo, indu*, a Prep. compounded of *in* (older *en*, cf. Gk. ἐν) and a lost Prep. *do* (cf. *dōnec*). See my *Hist. Gram.* ch. viii. § 18. Notice how the Prep. stands between the Adj. and Noun, **Ioueis at deiuos** (*Hist. Gram.* ch. viii. § 1), and follows its Pronoun, **ted endo** (cf. *mecum, tecum*), but precedes its Noun when no Adj. is used, **en Manom.** On **sied,** see *Hist. Gram.* ch. vi. § 13. **asted** for **adst-**. Already at this early period the group *dst* is reduced to *st*, though grammatical purists at a later age restored the full form of the Prep. in these compounds. **Noisi** is difficult to explain. The true precursor of Class. Lat. *nĭsĭ* (*nĭsī*) would be *nesei*. **Ope.** Why **Ope** and **pakari** should not have the final *m* expressed in writing, while **Manom** and **einom** have, is hard to say, unless the reason lay in the consonant-initial of the following word *t-, v-*, while **Manom** is followed by a vowel-initial and **einom** is 'in pausa,' at the end of a sentence.

Toitĕsiai. On **oi,** later *ū*, see § 7. The Gen. ending is disyllabic, *-āī*; see § 10.

The Beginning of Literature.

pakari. The explanation of this word is very doubtful. **uois**, supposed to be Class. Lat. *vīs*.

Duěnos. For *-os* see § 2. Pronounce *du-* like our *dw-* (see above). **fēkēd.** On the termination see § 8. **ěn**, see § 14. **Mānom.** On the termination see § 2. The stem *măno-* stands to the stem *māni-* of *Manes*, *immanis* as *săcro-* of *sacer* to *săcri-* of *porci sacres* 'pigs for sacrifice' (Plaut.). **einom.** The exact relation of this word to *enim* is not clear. The true representative of **einom** would be in Class. Lat. *īnum*. **dienoine**, a Locative, the *-e* of **noine** apparently representing the diphthong *ei* (§ 8). The two words **die** and **noine** form one word-group, to judge from the remark of Aulus Gellius (x. 24. 7): 'diequinte' et 'diequinti' pro adverbio copulate dictum est, secunda in eo syllaba correpta. See my *Hist. Gram.* ch. ii. § 11. **statod.** On the *-d* see *Hist. Gram.* ch. vi. § 14.

We may eke out these scanty remains of the very earliest period with the corrupt and uncertain fragments of some religious hymns, which belong to the same remote stage of antiquity:—

III. The Carmen Arvale, inscribed among the Acta Collegii Fratrum Arvalium of 218 A.D., discovered at Rome. (*C.I.L.* I. 28.)

1. enos Lases iuuate.
   enos Lases iuuate.
   enos Lases iuuate.

2. neue lue rue Marmar sins incurrere in pleoris.
   neue lue rue Marmar sins incurrere in pleoris.
   neue lue rue Marmar sins incurrere in pleoris.

3. satur fu fere Mars limen sali sta berber.
   satur fu fere Mars limen sali sta berber.
   satur fu fere Mars limen sali sta berber.

4. semunis alternei aduocapit conctos.
   semunis alternei aduocapit conctos.
   semunis alternei aduocapit conctos.

5. enos Marmor iuuato.
   enos Marmor iuuato.
   enos Marmor iuuato.

6. triumpe.
   triumpe.
   triumpe.
   triumpe.
   triumpe.

Neither the reading nor the sense of the above is at all certain. The Carmen Arvale was probably like the Carmina Saliaria 'vix sacerdotibus suis satis intellecta' (Quintilian, i. 6. 40); and the difficulty is increased for us by the fact that the workman who has carved the inscription has made a number of blunders, which we have to emend as best we can. The subjoined rendering is therefore only tentative:—

1. *nos(?), Lares, juvate.* 2. *neve luem, ruem, Marmar, sine incurrere in plures.* 3. *satur esto, fere Mars. limen sali, siste verber.* 4. *semones alternatim advocabit cunctus.* 5. *nos(?), Marmor, juvato.* 6. *triumphe!*

How much of all this is genuine Early Latin, and how much is the mere jingling perversion of old phrases by

priests who did not understand them, it is difficult to
say. The mere fact that **Lases** (with *s* retained between
vowels) and **pleoris** (with intervocalic *s* turned to *r*) occur
in the same inscription shews us that it has not been
preserved unchanged.

enos. The very first word offers a difficulty. It is
generally rendered *nos*. But the parallel of (ἐ)μέ in
Greek from the root (e)mo- does not quite warrant the
inference of (e)*no* in Latin from the root of the 1st Plur.
Pron. Perhaps **enos iuuate** represents *en nos iuuate*, i.e.
*injuvate nos (cf. *adjuvate nos*). On the Tmesis see *Hist.
Gram.* ch. vii. § 1, and on the absence of double consonants in early writing, § 17.

lue(m) rue(m), Acc. Sg. of Verbal Nouns from *luo* and
ruo, *lues* and *rues*. The Asyndeton, *luem ruem* for *luem
et ruem*, is a feature of Ante-classical Latin. **sins** is generally explained as an athematic 2d Sg. of *sino* with
Imperative sense, often called 'Injunctive' (cf. Gr. δό-ς).
Marmar is apparently some reduplicated form of the
name Mars. The forms **Mars** and **Marmor** also occur in
the hymn, and the variation looks like a piece of genuine
ancient usage. For we know from passages like Horace
(*S.* ii. 6. 20; *C. S.* 15–16) how important it was regarded
to address a deity on each occasion by the fitting name:—

(*S.* ii. 6. 20) Matutine pater seu Jane libentius audis.
(*C. S.* 15–16) sive tu Lucina probas vocari, Seu Genitalis.

When the consonant *r* occurred in two neighbouring
syllables of a word, one *r* was often dropped, e.g. *in-
creb(r)esco*, *praest(r)igiae*. Hence *Mā(r)mers*.

pleoris is certainly the spelling of the carver, but the form that preceded Class. Lat. *plures* was *ploer-* (not *pleor-*), the earlier stage of which was *plois-* (§§ 6, 7). **fu** is athematic 2d Sg. Imperative of O. Lat. *fuo*, whence Class. Lat. *fui* (*Hist. Gram.* ch. vi. § 8). **limen sali** seems to be merely *limen sali* 'leap over the threshold'; and **sta berber** is perhaps a mere Late Latin misspelling of **sta verber**, 'stay thy scourge.' The translation *sta fervere* 'desist from raging,' or better (with the active use of *stare*, p. 20, above) 'cause raging to stop,' leaves us to explain how **berber** can represent Class. Lat. *fervēre* or O. Lat. *fervĕre*. **Semunis** is generally equated with the *semones aut semideos* mentioned by Martianus Capella (ii. 156), *semo* apparently standing for *sēmi-homo* (cf. *nēmo*). Another rendering is 'the Sowers' (cf. *sēmen*). **alternei** is Loc. Sg. used as an Adverb 'alternately,' like *alternis* (Loc. Plur.) in Virg. **aduocapit** differs from Class. Lat. *advocabit* only in its *p* instead of *b*. **conctos** is Nom. Sg. Masc. On the termination see § 2, and on *-onc-* for Class. Lat. *-unc-* § 14. **triumpe**. The use of *ph* is not found till the end of the Republic (§ 23).

IV. The Carmina Saliaria, we have seen, were styled by Quintilian 'vix sacerdotibus suis satis intellecta.' Horace speaks of them in the same way (Epp. ii. 1. 86):—

  iam Saliare Numae carmen qui laudat et illud,
  quod mecum ignorat, solus uolt scire uideri.

We have a few scanty fragments preserved by the quotation of Grammarians, fragments of doubtful text and still more doubtful meaning, such as the following:[1]

(a) diuom †empta (? *leg.* patrem) cante, diuom deo supplicate.

divorum patrem (?) canite, divorum deo (? deum) supplicate.

This is a line from the Hymn to Janus. Cante seems to be a syncopated form of *canite*; cf. *caldus*, a by-form of *calidus*, current at the end of the Republican period.

(b) . . . Sancus Ianis es, duonus Cerus es, duonus Ianusque †pomeliosum recum.

Sancus Janis es, bonus Cerus es, bonus Janusque — meliorum regum.

This is another line from the Janus Hymn.

Ianis is a by-form of *Janus*, as *Manes* Plur. is of *Manus* (No. 2). On **duonus** see *Hist. Gram.* p. 155. **Cerus**, connected with *creo*, is explained by Roman Grammarians as *creator*. The same word, or a word from the same root, appears in dialectal divinity-names like *Cerfo-, Cerso-,* etc. On the *s* of *-meliosum* see § 6. The first syllable may be the old Preposition *pŏ* (cf. Gk. ἀπό), a by-form of *ab*, seen in *po-situs, po-lio, po-lūbrum,* a wash-basin (*Hist. Gram.* ch. vii. § 2). **recum**. On *c* for *g* see § 8.

(c) †quomne tonas, Leucesie, prai tet tremonti . . .

cum tonas, Lūcesie, praetremunt te.

quomne, an old form of *cum* (*quom*) augmented by the particle *-ne*. The *eu* of **Leucesie** (connected with *lux*) is

---

[1] I mark the specially doubtful words with an obelus.

strange, for I.-Eur. *eu* became *ou* in Latin. **Tet** is a way of writing *ted*, like *at* for *ad*, p. 22. In **tremonti** we have apparently the oldest form of the 3d Plur. *-ŏnti* (cf. Dor. Gk. -οντι, Att. -ουσι), which became, with loss of final *-i*, *tremont*, then *tremunt* (§ 14). In Early Latin an enclitic Pronoun, etc., was placed between the Prep. and the Verb in a Compound Verb, e.g. *prae te tremunt* for *praetremunt te*, *sub vos placo* for *supplico vos*, *ob vos sacro* for *obsecro vos*.

(*d*) pilumnoe poploe (? *leg.* pilumnoi poploi).

pilumni populi.

This is an epithet of the Romans, 'the javelin-armed tribes.'

Pilumnoi is Nom. Plur. in *-oi* (§ 10) of a word derived from *pilum*, a javelin. *Poplo-* is a by-stem of *populo-*.

Vases, mirrors, and jewel-boxes found at Praeneste, which date from the fourth century onwards, have early Latin inscriptions of a dialectal type. (*C.I.L.* I. 43 sqq.; XIV. 4094 sqq.)

V. Praenestine Vases:—

(*a*) Belolai pocolom. (*d*) Volcani pocolom.
   Bellulae poculum.   Vulcani poculum.

(*b*) Lauernai pocolom. (*e*) Aisclapi pocolom.
   Lavernae poculum.   Aesculapii poculum.

(*c*) Saeturni pocolom. (*f*) Salutes pocolom.
   Saturni poculum.   Salutis poculum.

These are all (except possibly the first) vases belonging to temples, and inscribed with the name of the deity to whose temple they belonged. In the *Rudens* of Plautus there is a mention of *sacra urna Veneria*, a vessel belonging to the temple of Venus, and inscribed with the name of the goddess. Sceparnio, who has been helping one of the attendants at the temple to draw water, finds himself left alone with the vessel in his possession, and is afraid he may get into trouble (v. 478): —

> nam haec litteratast, eapse cantat cuja sit.
> "for it is lettered and itself proclaims its owner's name."

On the Genitive terminations, see § 10. *Saeturno-* is the older form of the name of the god *Sāturno-*, found also in the Saliar Hymns, according to Festus: qui deus in Saliaribus Saeturnus nominatur, videlicet a sationibus. *Aisclapio-* is Class. Lat. *Aesculapius* (Dor. Gk. Ἀσκλαπιός).

VI. Praenestine Mirrors: —

(a) Uenos Diouem Prosepnai.
   Venus Jovem Proserpinae
   (sc. *conciliat*).

(b) Mirqurios Alixentrom.
   Mercurius Alexandrum.

(c) Poloces Losna Amuces.
   Pollux, Luna, Amycus.

(d) Castor Amucos Polouces.
   Castor, Amycus, Pollux.

(e) Iuno Iouei Hercele.
   Juno Jovi Herculem.

(f) Oanumede Diespater Cupido Menerua.
   Ganymedes, Jupiter, Cupido, Minerva.

The backs of these bronze mirrors have figures of deities, with the name written beside each figure. We thus get an interesting glimpse at the early popular (apparently dialectal) names of the Greek deities. *Prosepnā-* is nearer the Dor. Gk. Περσεφόνᾱ than the Class. Lat. *Proserpina*, which has been altered on the false analogy of *proserpo*. The Dative case **Prosepnai** was at one time read as **Prosepnais**, a curl of the goddess' hair being mistaken for the letter *s*. Hence in some text-books the imaginary "Gen. Sg. of the 1st Decl. in *-ais*." **Mirqurios** is with its *i* for *e* a dialectal form like Rustic Latin *stircus* for *stercus* (see No. 33). **Alixentrom** with its *tr* probably represents the actual pronunciation, for the group *dr* seems to have become *tr* in Latin, e.g. *ātro-* for **ādro-*, *nŭtrix* for **nŭdrix*, etc. (but *quadra*, etc.). **Poludouces* would be the earliest representative on Latin soil of Πολυδεύκης (on *ou* for *eu*, see § 7); then, with Syncope of the second syllable (§ 3), **Poldouces*, which would become *Pollouces*, the **Polouces** of (*d*) (on *l* for *ll*, see § 17). The *o* of **Poloces** of (*c*) is a dialectal equivalent of *ou*. **Losna** has the same dialectal *o* for *ou*. The original form would be **Louxna*, whence has come the Class. Lat. *Lūna* (§ 22). On the *c* of **Canumede**, see § 8. **Menerua**, probably still a quadrisyllable, was originally **Menes-uā* (§ 6), the vowel of the first syllable being afterwards changed perhaps by false analogy of *minor*, 'the lesser deity.'

VII. Praenestine jewel-boxes (*cistae*).

(*a*) **Dindia Macolnia fileai dedit.**

Dindia Magulnia filiae dedit.

Nouios Plautios med Romai fecid.

Novius Plautius me Romae fecit.

The Beginning of Literature.   31

The different spelling of the terminations of **dedit** and **fecid** is curious. **Fileai** is perhaps dialectal for *filiaî*. On **med** see § 19, and on **Romai** (Locative), class. *Romae*, § 7.

These jewel-boxes usually have elaborate carving on the lid, sometimes with names indicating the personages delineated. Among these early (dialectal) forms of the names of gods and heroes found on Praenestine cistae may be mentioned: **Aciles** *Achilles*, **Tondrus** *Tyndareus*, **Acmemeno** *Agamemnon*, **pater poumilionom** *pater pumilionum*, 'the father of the dwarfs' (on -*om* Gen. Plur. see § 2), **Oinumama** *Unimamma*, 'an Amazon.'

A Praenestine cista (probably later in date than others) in a French collection has a curious kitchen scene, with words attributed to the various personages engaged in cooking (*Mélanges d'Archéologie*, 1890, p. 303):—

(*b*) feri porod   cofeci   made mi recie
   feri porro   *confeci*   *made (? -t) mi regie*
   'strike away'   'I have done'   'boil (? it boils) nobly for me'

   misc sane   asom fero   confice piscim
   misce sane   *assum (arsum) fero*   *confice piscem*
   'yes! give me wine'   'I am carrying this to the fire'   'get the fish done'

the whole being entitled **coenalia**, *cenalia* Neut. Plur., 'a dinner scene.'

The variety of spelling between **cofeci** and **confice** (§ 22), **porod**, **recie**, and **sane** (§ 19) is probably not due to mere carelessness of orthography, but represents the tendencies of the pronunciation of the day. On the single *r* of **porod**, see § 17, and on the Ablatival *d*, § 10. If **misc** is not a miswriting for *misce*, it must come from a 3d Conj. *misco, Imperat. *miscĕ* (on the dropping of final *ĕ*, see below, § 21). On the single *s* of **asom**, see § 17, and on -*om*, § 2. **Piscim** shews the true Acc. ending of I-stems, often altered to the -*em* of Cons. Stems (*Hist. Gram.* ch. iii. § 8). The spelling **coenalia** is interesting, for it proves that even at this early period the Latin *cena* had been wrongly connected with the Greek κοινός.

VIII. Dedicatory inscription from the grove of Diana at Nemi. (*C.I.L.* xiv. 4182 *a*.)

> Diana M. Livio M. f. praitor dedit.
>
> *Dianae M. Livius M(arci) f(ilius) praetor dedit.*

On the Dat., **Diana**, see § 10. Final -*s* is often omitted in the Nom. Sg. of IO-stems on early inscriptions. It seldom lengthens a short syllable by 'position' in Early Latin Poetry (§ 20). Final -*m* was at all times weakly pronounced, so that it merely nasalized the preceding vowel. It is often omitted on early inscriptions, as well as on late (§§ 20, 27).

IX. On lip of bronze vase. (*Ephemeris Epigraphica*, ii. 299.)

> Q. Lainio Q. f. praifectos protrebibos fecit.
>
> *Q. Laenius Q. f. praefectus pro tribubus fecit.*

The writing of the Prep. along with its Noun, pro-trebibos, corresponded to the pronunciation, for Prep. and Noun formed a single word-group. It was the practice down to late times (see my *Hist. Gram.* ch. ii. § 11). The classical spelling *tribubus* did not express the sound in the classical period of the second syllable, but was a grammarian's device to distinguish, e.g. *arcubus* 4th Decl. from *arcibus* 3d Decl. The spelling here with *i* seems to shew that the weakening of unaccented *u* to *i* (§ 14) had begun early. On the ending *-bŏs* of the Dat. Plur. see § 2.

X. A dedication-tablet, found near Praeneste. (*C.I.L.* I. 187.)

M. Mindios L. fi. P. Condetios Va. fi. aidiles uicesma parti Apolones dederi.

M. Mindius L. fi., P. Conditius Va(lerii) fi. aediles vice-simam partem Apollinis ("belonging to Apollo") *dederi* (sc. *aedi*).

uicesma(m), with its Syncope of the penultimate vowel, is not a pure Latin form. **parti(m)**. On this old Acc. of *pars*, preserved in the Adverb *partim* (cf. *maximam partem* used adverbially), see above, § 10. **Apolōnes** (on *l* for *ll* see § 17) preserves the Greek declension of the name, like *Castŏris*. On the Gen. termination *-ĕs*, see § 10. If **dederi** be a true form, the *-ĕ* of Class. Lat. *dedere* must have come from an original *ī*. (On dialectal *dedro* 'dederunt,' see No. 29, below.)

XI. Dedicatory inscription found in Picenum. (*C.I.L.* I. 181.)

L. Terentio L. f. L. Aprufenio O. f. L. Turpilio O. f. M. Albani L. f. T. Munatio T. f. quaistores aire moltaticod dederont.

L. Terentius . . . M. Albanius . . . quaestores aere multatico (from the money raised by fines) *dederunt*.

On the Abl. forms **airĕ** and **moltaticōd** see § 10. The Nom. Sg. **Albani(s)** represents a common declension of IO-stems (*Hist. Gram.* ch. iii. § 6). On the dropping of final *s* see § 20, and on the *o* of *molta-*, § 15.

XII. On a small pillar found at Tusculum. (*C.I.L.* I. 63.)

M. Fourio O. f. tribunos militare de praidad Maurte dedet.

M. Fūrius C(aii) f(ilius) tribunus militaris de praeda Marti dedit.

The loss of final *-s* in **Fourio** (on the diphthong see § 7) and **militare** shews the tendency of the pronunciation of the day (see below, § 20). **praidad** shews the old *d* termination of the Abl. Sg. (§ 10) and the diphthong *ai* (§ 7). Whether **Maurte** is meant for *Mavurte*, i.e. *Māvorti*, or represents a vowel sound which became *ā* in *Mārti*, is hard to say. On the *-et* of **dedet**, a spelling of *-eit*, as the *-te* of *Maurte* is of *-tei*, see § 8.

XIII. On a dedicatory bronze plate found at Nemi. (*C.I.L.* XIV. 4269.)

O. Manlio Aci. . . . cosol pro poplo Ariminesi.

C. Manlius Aci(dinus) consul pro populo Ariminensi.

This is not the consul of 179 B.C., but a magistrate (*consul*) of Ariminum. The lettering of the dedication is ancient; but an Abl. like *poplo* without final *d* is not a feature of inscriptions of this time (see on No. 34).

A mark of inscriptions belonging to the close of the second century is the use of *u* for the older *o* in final syllables. Examples of the encroachment of the younger form are:—

XIV. Dedicatory inscription, found at Rome. (*Not. Scav.* 1890, p. 10.)

. . . [Tre]bonius Q. f. Numisio Martio donom dedit meretod.

. . . *Trebonius Q. f. Numisio Martio donum dedit merito.*

Notice [**Tre**]**bonius** with *u* beside **donom** with *o*. **Numisio** is a dialectal form, the true Latin equivalent being *Numerius* (see on No. 7, above). On the *e* of **meretod** and the Abl. -*d* see §§ 14, 19.

XV. Dedicatory inscription, companion to the above. (*C.I.L.* I. 190.)

Numisio Martio M. Terebonio C. l. donum dat libens meritod.

Numisio Martio M. Trebonius C. l(ibertus) donum dat libens merito.

The *i* of **libens** and **meritod** are spellings which did not come into general use till a later time. On this, the inscription of a freedman, they are not inconsistent with antiquity. The spelling **Terebonio** with parasitic vowel between *t* and *r* is another mark of plebeian authorship.

XVI. Dedicatory inscriptions on a pillar found at Praeneste. (*C.I.L.* xiv. 2891–3.)

(a) L. Gemenio L. f. Pel. Hercole dono et dat lubs merto pro sed sueque ede leigibus ara Salutus.

L. Geminius L. f. Pel(igna, sc. *tribu) Herculi donum: et dat libens merito pro se suisque eisdem legibus* ('on the same conditions') *aram Salutis.*

(b) Q. K. Cestio Q. f. Hercole donu dedero.

Q. (et) K(aeso) Cestius Q. f(ilii) Herculi donum dederunt.

Both these inscriptions have dialectal deflections from pure Latin; **lubs** should be *lubes* (on *es* for *ens*, see § 22); **merto** should be *mereto*; **sueque** and **ede** should be *suesque, esde* (?); **leigibus** should probably be *legibus*, and **dedero**, *dederont* (cf. No. 29 below).

On the *o* of **Hercole**, see § 14. Throughout the inscription the diphthong *ei* is written *e* (§ 8). On **sed**, see § 19, and on *-us* (older *-os*) of **Salutus**, § 10. For **Cestio** (apparently *Cestiōs*, Nom. Sg.) we should expect the Nom. Plur., according to the Latin usage. Notice the intrusion of the 'modern' *u* (§ 14) in **leigibus, donu**(m).

XVII. Dedicatory inscription, found in the sacred grove of Diana at Nemi. (*C.I.L.* xiv. 4270.)

Poublilia Turpilia Cn. uxor hoce seignum pro Cn. filiod Dianai donum dedit.

Publilia Turpilia Cn. uxor hoc signum pro Cn. filio Dianae donum dedit.

On the *ou* of **Poublilia**, see § 7. **Hoce** for *hocce* (§ 7), a form preserved in the Class. Lat. interrogative *hoccīne*, (for *hoccĕ-ne*, § 14). The double consonant is still written single (§ 17). The *ei* of **seignum** perhaps indicates merely the *ē*-sound which *ĭ* (cf. *sĭgillum*) received before *gn*. (See my *Latin Language*, ch. ii. § 144.) On **filiod**, see § 19, and on **Dianai͡**, § 7.

XVIII. Dedicatory inscription. (Cagnat, *L'Année Épigraphique*, 1890, No. 85.)

Aiscolapio donom L. Albanius K. f. dedit.
Aesculapio donum L. Albanius K. f. dedit.

For **Aiscolapio** cf. the note on *Aisclapi* of No. 5 e.

Two nearly contemporary inscriptions, whose date can be fixed, differ in their spelling of *-os, -om*, etc.

XIX. Dedicatory inscription on an altar found at Rome; 217 B.C. (*C.I.L.* I. 1503.)

Hercolei sacrom M. Minuci C. f. dictator uouit.
Herculi sacrum. M. Minucius C. f. dictator vovit.

Minuci is the Nom. Sg. form of *Minucio-* that was used in ordinary speech, where also *Minucim* replaced *Minucium* (cf. *Albani*, No. 11). On the *o* of **Hercolei, sacrom**, see § 14; and on the Dat. Sg. ending *-ei*, § 5.

XX. Found at Rome; c. 211 B.C. (*C.I.L.* I. 530.)

M. Claudius M. f. consol Hinnad cepit.
M. Claudius M. f. consul ex Henna cepit.

Livy (xxiv. 39) tells us of the capture of Henna, in Sicily, by M. Claudius Marcellus. The use of the double consonant in the spelling of the town's name is interesting, for it is the earliest example of this practice on a Latin inscription (§ 17); though it is hardly a fair example, since it may be a mere reproduction of the Greek mode of spelling the name. The reason why *Hinna*, and not *Hĕnna*, is written is not clear. Possibly the *i* reflects the Greek pronunciation of ε as close *e*. (But cf. *didit*, No. 22, and see the remark on No. 24.)

The variation, *-us* and *-ol*, reappears in another inscription of the same consul: —

XXI. Found at Rome; c. 211 B.C. (*C.I.L.* I. 531.)

Martei M. Claudius M. f. consol dedit.
Marti M. Claudius M. f. consol dedit.

It is also seen in an inscription of 200 B.C.

XXII. Found in the sacred grove of Diana at Nemi. (*C.I.L.* XIV. 4268.)

C. Aurilius C. f. praitor iterum didit eisdim consol probavit.
C. Aurelius C. f. praetor iterum dedit; idem consul probavit.

The *ĭ* of **Aurilius** may exemplify that change of *ĕ* to *ĭ* seen in *delinio* for *delenio*, etc. (*Hist. Gram.* ch. ii. § 15; B. *App.* § 90.) On **eisdim**, see § 22.

XXIII. On a dedicatory bronze plate, found at Tibur, we have two inscriptions, one with *-us, -u(m)* for *-os, -om*, apparently somewhat later than the other (*C.I.L.* I. 62).

(a) O. Placentios Her. f. Marte sacrom.
  C. Placentius Her(ii) f. Marti sacrum.
(b) O. Placentius Her. f. Marte donu dede.
  C. Placentius Her. f. Marti donum dedit.

On **donu** and **dede**, see § 20.

The same change is noticeable on the Scipio epitaphs, the three of which that belong to the third century I arrange in order of probable priority.[1]

XXIV. Epitaph of L. Cornelius Scipio, consul 259 B.C. (*C.I.L.* I. 31.)

  L. Cornelio L. f. Scipio aidiles cosol cesor.
  L. Cornelius L. f. Scipio aedilis consul censor.

The *-les* for *-lis* in **aidiles** and the *e* of *Tempestatebus* in No. 25 are due to the confusion between $\breve{e}$ and $\breve{i}$ at this period when unaccented $\breve{e}$ was passing into $\breve{i}$ (§ 14).

XXV. Epitaph of the same. (*C.I.L.* I. 32.)
  hone oino ploirume cosentiont Romai
  duonoro optumo fuise uiro
  Luciom Scipione filios Barbati
  consol censor aidilis hic fuet apud uos
  hec cepit Corsica Aleriaque urbe
  dedet Tempestatebus aide meretod.

  hunc unum plurimi consentiunt Romae
  bonorum optimum fuisse virum
  Lucium Scipionem: filius Barbati

---

[1] There is no reason to believe that each Scipio epitaph belongs to the date of the decease of the Scipio it commemorates.

consul, censor, aedilis hic fuit apud vos:
hic cepit Corsicam Aleriamque urbem:
dedit Tempestatibus aedem merito.

oino(m) (on the diphthong see § 7) is the same formation as Gk. οἴνη the ace, Engl. 'one,' from the same root as Gk. οἶος, alone. **ploirume** Nom. Plur. Masc. (on *-e* for *-ei* see § 8) shews the old form of Class. Lat. *plurimo-*, the still older form of which had *plois-*, not *ploir-* (see my *Hist. Gram.* ch. iv. § 3). **cosentiont** retains the *o* of the termination which soon after this time became *-unt* (§ 2). **Romaî** is Locative (§ 7). **duonoro(m)**. *duono-* is the old form of the stem *bono-*, found also in Livius Andronicus' Odyssey:—

    simul duona eorum portant ad nauis

(see above, p. 20, on the name *Dueno-*, and for the change of *du-* to *b-*, *Hist. Gram.* ch. x. § 13). The Gen. Plur. ending *-orom*, earlier *-ōsōm*, and later *-ōrŭm*, belonged at first to Pronouns only, but was extended to Adjectives (as **duonoro** here), and from Adjectives to Nouns, until it finally expelled altogether the true Noun and Adj. ending *-ōm*, later *-um* (*Hist. Gram.* ch. iii. § 6). **uiro** may be Gen. Plur. with this true Noun ending or Acc. Sg. Livy (xxix. 14. 8) tells us that this title was conferred by the Senate in 204 B.C. on P. Scipio Nasica: (judicaverunt eum esse) *virum bonorum optimum*. **consol censor**. Notice the retention of *n* before *s* in contrast with **cosentiont** v. 1 and of **cosol cesor** of No. 24. The uncertainty about the spelling of such words is seen also in **cofeci** and **confice** of No. 7 *b*. **fuet**. On *e* see § 8.

hĕc. The Pronoun is here emphatic, and retains the form unweakened by loss of accent (§ 14), while in v. 4 it has the unaccented form hĭc. **Corsica(m) Aleria(m)que urbe(m)** 'Corsica and Aleria its chief town.'

This campaign of Scipio's is mentioned by several historians, e.g. Livy, *Epit.* 17, *L. Cornelius consul in Sardinia et Corsica contra Sardos et Corsos et Hannonem Poenorum ducem feliciter pugnavit.* Aleria is the Roman form of the Greek name Ἀλαλία with *l-r* for *l-l* (*Hist. Gram.* ch. ii. § 8; B. *App.* § 99) and with Vowel-weakening in the second syllable, § 2.

meretod. On *e* in the second syllable see § 14; and on the Abl. *-d*, § 10.

XXVI. Epitaph of L. Cornelius Scipio Barbatus; consul 298 B.C. (*C.I.L.* I. 30.)

Cornelius Lucius Scipio Barbatus
Gnaiuod patre prognatus fortis uir sapiensque
quoius forma uirtutei parisuma fuit
consol censor aidilis quei fuit apud uos
Taurasia Cisauna Samnio cepit
subigit omne Loucanam opsidesque abdoucit.[1]

Cornelius Lucius Scipio Barbatus,
Gnaeo patre prognatus fortis vir sapiensque,
cujus forma virtuti parissima fuit,
consul, censor, aedilis qui fuit apud vos,
Taurasiam, Cisaunam, Samnium cepit,
subigit omnem Lucanam obsidesque abducit.

[1] It is possible that **abdoucit** has been corrected to **abdoucsit** (*abduxit*) on the stone.

In the first line we seem to have left the region of Early Latin and to find ourselves in the Classical Age, for -ŏs has been replaced by -us in the termination of the Nom. Sg., ou by ū in the name *Lucius*. But traces of the earlier spelling remain in the other lines. **Gnaiuod**. The father's name is given in the antique form, though a still older spelling had the letter *C* instead of *G* (§ 8), whence the contraction, prevalent even in the Classical Age, *Cn.* for *Gnaeus*, like *C.* for *Gaius*. On the diphthong *ai* see § 7; on the *v*, lost in the Classical form *Gnae(v)us*, § 14; and on Abl. -*d*, § 19. **patrĕ** is the Locative, originally *patrĭ* (§ 10), which in the 3d Decl. usurped the place of the Ablative in Consonant Stems. On **quoius** see § 10, and on **uirtutei** § 3. **parisuma**. The Superlative of *par* is rare. We find it also in a line of Plautus (*Curc* 506):—

eodem hercle vos pono et paro: parissumi estis hibus,

along with two other rare forms, the verb *păro, -are*, I make equal, I equate, and O. Lat. *hībus* for *his* Dat. Abl. Translate: "indeed I put you in the same box and count you alike: you are exactly like them." **quei** with the weakened form of the diphthong, a form belonging to the unaccented use of the Relative (§ 3), whereas in the Dvenos inscription (No. 2) we had the unweakened form *quoi* (written *qoi*). **Samnio** may be Abl., "took T. and C. from Samnium," in which case one Ablative of the inscription, **Gnaiuod**, would have the old *d*-termination, while the other lacked it. But it may also be Accusative with *omne* supplied from the next line: *omne Samnium, omnem Lucanam*.

Notice that final -*m* is dropped in this inscription when the next word begins with a consonant.

Taurasia and Cisauna were apparently towns in Samnium.

Loucanam, sc. *terram.*

opsides. On the spelling *ps* see *Hist. Gram.* ch. ii. § 10. **Abdoucit.** The *ū* of Class. Lat. *dūco* represents the early diphthong eu, which became in Latin *ou* (§ 7); for the Indo-European form of the verb was *deuco (Germ. ziehe, Goth. tiuha).

XXVII. Epitaph on the son of Scipio Africanus Major. (*C.I.L.* i. 33.)

quei apice insigne Dialis flaminis gesistei
Mors perfecit tua ut essent omnia breuia
honos fama uirtusque gloria atque ingenium
quibus sei in longa licuiset tibe utier uita
facile facteis superases gloriam maiorum.
qua re lubens te in gremiu Scipio recipit
terra Publi prognatum Publio Corneli.

qui apicem, insigne Dialis flaminis, gessisti,
Mors perfecit tua ut essent omnia brevia,
honos, fama virtusque, gloria atque ingenium;
quibus si in longa licuisset tibi uti vita,
facile factis superasses gloriam majorum.
quare libens te in gremium, Scipio, recipit
terra, Publi, prognatum Publio, Corneli.

I place this epitaph here in order to keep it beside the other Scipio Epitaphs, though it is probably a good deal later. It has few features of antiquity except the avoidance of writing a double consonant in **gesistei, licuiset**, and **superases** (but **essent**). The diphthong *ei*, **quei** (p. 42), **gesistei, sei, facteis** (§ 5), has not yet passed into *ī* (§ 7). In **tibe** the *e* may be the old method of writing *ei* (§ 8), but is more likely to be *ĕ*, a substitute for *ī* (§ 21).

The following ancient inscriptions from the grove of Pisaurum may find a place here, at the close of this section. They cannot be called pure Latin inscriptions, but represent rather the dialectal variety spoken in Picenum, with final *s* dropped even after a long vowel, and with clipped form of the 3d Plur. ending of Verbs. (*C.I.L.* I. 167 sqq.):—

XXVIII. Iunone re[gina] matrona Pisaurese dono dedrot.
  Junoni reginae matronae Pisaurenses dono dederunt.

matronā(s) is the dialectal Nom. Plur. of the 1st Decl., which in Latin was superseded by the Pronominal Plural in *-ai* (see my *Hist. Gram.* ch. iii. § 4). It drops final *-s* like **Pisauresē(s)**.

XXIX. Matre Matuta dono dedro matrona M'. Ouria Pola Liuia deda.
  Matri Mātūtae dono dederunt matronae, M(ania) Curia Polla Livia dederunt.

On the Dat. **Matuta**, see § 10. **deda(nt)** is some dialectal *ā*-Preterite like Lat. *erā-s, dabā-s*, etc. (see my *Hist. Gram.* ch. vi. § 8). Like **dedro(nt)** it drops final *-nt*.

XXX.   (a) Deiu[os] Nouesede.
   (b) T. Popaio Pop. f.
   (a) *Divi Novensiles.*
   (b) *T. Poppaeus Pub(lii) j.*

Deiuos is Nom. Plur. (with the dialectal ending *-ōs*) like **Nouesĕdē(s)**. The latter shews *-es-* for *-ens-* (§ 22).

The inscription on the Columna Rostrata also deserves a place here. For though in its present form it is a restoration made at the time of the Emperor Claudius, it doubtless retains a great deal of the old inscription, and is appealed to by Quintilian as evidence of Early Latin (*Inst.* i. 7. 12, Latinis veteribus 'd' plurimis in verbis adjectum ultimum, quod manifestum est etiam ex columna rostrata, quae est Duellio in foro posita). A good deal of it is lost. (*C.I.L.* I. 195):—

XXXI. . . . nouem castreis exfociont Macelamque . . . pucnandod cepit enque eodem macistratud . . . rem nauebos marid consol primos . . . clasesque nauales primos ornauet . . . cumque eis nauebos claseis Poenicas omnis . . . maxumas copias Oartaciniensis praesented . . . dictatored olorom inaltod marid pucnandod . . . uique naueis cepet cum socieis septeresmom . . . triresmosque naueis . . . quoque naualed praedad poplom, etc.

[*post dies*] *novem castris effugiunt. Macellamque* [*vi*] *pugnando cepit, inque eodem magistratu* [*bene*] *rem navibus mari consul primus* [*gessit*], *classesque navales primus ornavit* [*paravitque*], *cumque eis navibus classes Punicas omnes,* [*item*] *maximas copias Carthaginienses praesente* (i.e. imperante) [*Hannibale*] *dictatore illorum in alto mari pugnando* [*vicit*], *vique naves cepit cum sociis, septiremem* [*unam quinqueremesque*] *triremesque naves*, . . . [*primus*] *quoque navali praeda populum* [*donavit*], etc.

Archaic features of the above are the use throughout of the letter C both for the sound *c* and the sound *g*, the expression of double consonants by single, the Abl. ending *-d* in **altod, marid, pucnandod,** etc., the use of *-que* for 'and' to the exclusion of *et* ('also'), the literal sense of **prae-sented** 'being in command,' the employment of *o, e* for the classical *ŭ, ĭ,* in *-ont* 3d Plur. *-bos* Abl. Plur., *-os* Nom. Sg., *-rom* Gen. Plur., *en* Prep.; also of *ei* for class. *ī* in **castreis, socieis,** and so on. But pseudo-archaisms are interspersed, e.g. **exfociont** for **exfuciont** (with Indo-European *ŭ*; cf. Gk. ἔφυγον), **dictatored** (cf. **praesented**) for *dictatore* (*-rī*) or *dictatorĭd* (§ 10). The termination of **praedad** is antique, but not the diphthong, which should be *ai* (§ 7) (cf. **praesented**).

Macella was a town in Sicily. The only instance of a Gen. Plur. of the 2d Decl. is **olorom** (i.e. *ollorom*), *illorum*, where the ending *-orom* is quite in place, the word being a Pronoun (p. 40). **inaltod.** Notice the writing of the Prep. along with its Adj. (cf. p. 32). **septeresmom** . . . **triresmosque.** The *esm* (class. *ēm*, § 22) is the ancient spelling; but whether the use of the Masc. form be a genuine ancient construction or an imitation of the Greek, is difficult to say. On **poplom** cf. No. 4 *d*.

CHAPTER II.

THE PERIOD OF THE REPUBLICAN LITERATURE.

16. The reduction of Diphthongs, even in the accented syllable, was steadily carried on throughout this period. *Ai* became *ae* about the beginning of the second century, though the older form is often retained, especially in state inscriptions, laws, and the like. *Ei* did not wholly sink to *ī* till about 150 B.C. On inscriptions previous to that time, such as the S. C. de Bacchanalibus (No. 37), a state inscription, and therefore carefully written, we find *ei* kept clearly separate from *ī*. The old expression of the diphthong *ei* by the letter *e* (§ 8) went out of use about the end of the third century B.C. *Ou* began to be pronounced and spelled *ū* about the same time, though this older spelling, too, is retained in laws and inscriptions of a ceremonious character. *Oi* became *oe*, as *ai* became *ae*, and passed in pronunciation into a simple vowel-sound, written *ū*, about the beginning of the second century. (For these and other changes see my *Hist. Gram.* ch. x. § 11.)

17. A result of the weakening of the diphthong *ei* to the sound *ī* was that the long vowel *ī* was often written *ei* for the sake of distinction from *ĭ* (e.g. No. 44). This practice came in about the middle of the second century and remained till the beginning of the Empire; though from the time of Sulla *ī* is usually indicated by a tall form of the letter, e.g. MENDICVS. The poet Accius (died c. 90 B.C.) introduced the practice of expressing the length of other vowels by writing them double, e.g. PAASTORES, SEEDEM, a practice which was retained for some time after his death. The doubling of consonants in writing had been previously brought into fashion by the poet Ennius, and continued ever afterwards to be the regular usage of Latin spelling.

18. Another affection that the language suffered in the course of this period was the shortening of certain long vowels when final or when preceding certain final consonants. Before final -*m* a long vowel had been shortened even earlier. The -*ōm* (Gk. -ων) of the Gen. Plur. had become -*ŏm*, which, being an unaccented syllable, was reduced to -*ŭm*. And final -*ā* had been shortened before the beginning of Roman literature in the Nom. Sg. of the 1st Decl., etc. In no extant Latin poetry is there any certain trace of the original quantity *terrā*, etc. (cf. Gk. χώρᾱ). Long vowels in final syllables were most readily shortened by Roman lips in iambic words, e.g. *fŭga* (Gk. φυγή, φυγά), where the short but accented first syllable exercised a shortening effect on the following long syllable. This law of Latin pronunciation is known as the Law of Breves Breviantes (*Hist. Gram.* ch. ii. § 16). So we may suppose that the shortening of final -*ā* began with iambic words like *fuga*, and from them gradually extended to all Nominatives of the 1st Decl. Plautus, whose poetry follows the

Republican Period.

ordinary, everyday pronunciation of actual life, usually employs shortened forms like *căvĕ, ăbĭ*, etc., especially of such words as would be rapidly uttered in discourse, e.g. Adverbs like *modo, probe* (cf. Class. Lat. *mălĕ, bĕnĕ*, never *mălē, bĕnē*). At a later period the shortening of final -*ō* was extended from words of Iambic form, e.g. *ĕo, vŏco, dăbo*, to all words, in precisely the same fashion as the shortening of -*ā* had been effected in the third century B.C. But this shortening of -*ō* was not fully accomplished till the Empire; cf. *estŏ*, etc., in Ovid.

This shortening of long vowels when final or when preceding a final consonant was another result of the Latin stress accentuation (§ 1). The final syllable being unaccented did not get its full and proper utterance. But the shortening was often aided by the character of the final consonant before which it stood. We ourselves find it difficult to give a vowel the same lengthened pronunciation before a final *t* as before a final *d*. We do not make the *o* of 'note' so long as the *o* of 'node.' To a Roman, too, final *t* exercised a shortening influence over a preceding long vowel; and by about the middle of the second century B.C. (posterior, that is to say, to the time of Plautus) we find the pronunciation established of *terrĕt* for older *terrēt* (cf. *terrēs*), *curăt* for older *curāt* (cf. *curās*), etc. Slightly later came the shortening of long vowels before final *r*, e.g. *curĕr* for older *curēr* (cf. *curēris*), *calcăr* from older *calcār* (originally *calcāre*, sc. *ferrum* 'the iron attached to the heel'), *oratŏr* for older *oratōr* (cf. *oratōris*, Gk. ῥήτωρ). *L* had the same shortening effect as *r*, as we see from *tribunăl* from *tribunāl(e)*, etc. That these consonants, however, did not produce this result wholly of themselves, but were helped by the unaccented nature of the final syllable, we can see from monosyllables like *păr*, *sŏl*, which being accented retain the long quantity.

19. Stress-accentuation must also have had something to do with an earlier phonetic change, the loss of final *d* after a long vowel, which took place about the beginning of the literary period. The Latin Abl. Sg. originally ended in *d*, e.g. *terrād*, *dolōd*, etc.; and in the elevated poetry of Livius Andronicus and Naevius there are traces of the older form of Abl. Thus a Saturnian line of Naevius has the Abl. *Troiād* 'from Troy':—

nóctu Troíad exíbant ‖ cápitibus opértis,

'they passed from Troy in the night, veiling their heads.' But there is probably no trace of it in Plautus, certainly none in his dialogue verses. On the S. C. de Bacchanalibus (No. 37) of 186 B.C., two years before the death of Plautus, it is invariably written, a practice quite in keeping with the archaic orthography of a state decree. On the earlier and less formal edict of Aemilius Paulus (No. 34) it is not found. By this loss of final *d* after a long vowel the Abl. Sg. of the Declensions came to end in *-ā*, *-ō*, *-ī*, *-ū*, *-ē*, instead of *-ād*, *-ōd*, *-īd*, *-ūd*, *-ēd*. Such Adverbs as were originally Ablative were similarly affected, e.g. *suprā(d)*, *extrā(d)*, *porrō(d)*, *facillimē(d)*. And *-tōd*, *-ntōd* of the 3d Sg. and 3d Plur. Imperat. were reduced to *-to*, *-nto*, e.g. *esto*, *sunto*. Monosyllables like the Acc. and Abl. of the Personal Pronouns *mēd*, *tēd*, *sēd*, retained their *d* longer, though the *d* has quite disappeared by the middle of the second century. On the other hand, *haud*, which in early literature appears as *haud* before an initial vowel and *hau* before an initial consonant (cf. our 'an' and 'a'), e.g. *haud ignoro, hau scio*, managed to retain its final *d* in the classical language.

20. The weak sound of a final consonant and its liability to be affected by a following initial consonant is reflected in the interchange which we find on inscriptions of all periods between final *t* and final *d*. The pronunciation would doubtless be, for example, *at templum*, etc., but *ad delubrum*, etc.; and in consequence we find the Prep. sometimes written *at*, sometimes *ad* (cf. *aput* and *apud, set* and *sed*); while in carelessly written inscriptions a final -*t* is often dropped, e.g. *dede* for *dedet* (= *dedeit*), class. *dedit* (No. 23). Final -*m* had a very weak pronunciation, shewing its presence, in fact, only in the nasal sound given to the preceding vowel, so that -*om* would have in Latin a sound like French 'on.' It is omitted again and again on the oldest, as on the Post-classical inscriptions. Final -*s* after a short vowel is scarcely allowed in the early poetry to give length by 'position' to its syllable when the next word begins with a consonant. Even Catullus in one epigram scans *tu dăbīs supplicium*, a scansion which we generally indicate by substituting an apostrophe for the *s*: *tu dabi' supplicium*. Cicero tells us that in his time the failure to give clear enunciation to a final *s* had come to be considered *subrusticum;* and this corrected pronunciation seems to have found its way into Vulgar Latin too, for the Romance languages shew traces of a final -*s*, e.g. Fr. sommes from Lat. *sumus*.

21. Final vowels, too, suffered from the stress on the initial syllable of the word. A final ĕ (which often has taken the place of a final ĭ, e.g. *tristĕ* for **tristĭ*, *mitĕ* for **mitĭ*; contrast Gk. ἴδρῐ, Neut. of I-stem) came to be dropped, especially in words which were in ordinary utterance closely joined with a following word; thus *neque* became *nec*, *atque* became *ac* (for **atc*), the Imperatives *dice*, *duce*, *face* became *dic*, *duc*, *fac*, etc. See my *Hist. Gram.* ch. ii. § 12.

22. Another change accomplished at this period is the change of *vŏ-* to *vĕ-*, e.g. *versus* for *vorsus*, *vester* for *voster*. Scipio Africanus Minor is said to have brought in the new fashion. Another was the loss of *g* in the initial group *gn*, e.g. *natus* for *gnatus*, which reminds us of our own loss of *k* in *kn-*, e.g. know (pronounced like 'no'), knee, etc. Plautus and Terence seem to use the spelling *gnatus* for the Noun, *natus* for the Participle.

The loss of *s*, with compensatory lengthening, before a voiced consonant was of earlier date, e.g. *dūmus* for *dŭsmus* (Liv. Andr. has *dusmo* (Adj.) *in loco*, 'in a bushy place'), *īdem* for *is-dem* (Cicero mentions this latter spelling. There was a similar treatment of *x* (= *cs*), e.g. *ēdīco* for *ĕx-dīco*. But in these compounds the original form was often restored from a sense of their etymology.

Similarly *n*, which was in pronunciation dropped before *s*, *f*, with lengthening of the vowel, was usually restored in the standard orthography, at least of Classical Latin; e.g. *consulo*, pronounced *cōsulo*, probably with nasalized ō.

Republican Period.

(A) Earlier Part.

This part is marked by the dropping of final *d* after a long vowel in writing, as it had been already dropped in pronunciation, and by the introduction of the double writing of double consonants.

XXXII. The Spoletium Inscription (a notice hung up in a sacred grove at Spoletium in Umbria). (*C.I.L.* xi. 4766.)

honce loucom nequis uiolatod neque exuehito neque exferto quod louci siet neque cedito nesei quo die res deina anua fiet. eod die quod reidinai causa fiat sine dolo cedere licetod. seiquis uiolasit Ioue bouid piaclum datod. seiquis scies uiolasit dolo malo Iouei bouid piaclum datod et a. CCC moltai suntod. eius piacli moltaique dicatore exactio estod.

hunc lucum nequis violato neque evehito neque efferto quod luci sit neque caedito, nisi quo die res divina annua fiet. Eo die quod rei divinae causa fiat sine dolo caedere liceto. Siquis violassit (violaverit), Jovi bove piaculum dato. Siquis sciens violassit (violaverit) dolo malo, Jovi bove piaculum dato et a(eris) CCC multae sunto. Ejus piaculi multaeque dicatori (?) exactio esto.

Here final -*d* after a long vowel is sometimes written, sometimes dropped, with no apparent method. Double consonants are still written single, e.g. **anua, uiolasit**. One form is dialectal and not genuine Latin, viz. **cedere** instead of *caidere;* for in the Umbrian dialect of Latin *ae* was already pronounced *e*, a pronunciation which in time affected the Latin of the capital and of the whole Roman world. (See the last section of this book.)

honce. The full form is suitable to a solemn notice of this kind, though in actual talk the final ĕ would be always dropped (§ 21). On ŏ for Class. Lat. ŭ, see § 14.

uiolatod. This Imperative ending -tōd is said to have been originally the Abl. Sg. of the Demonstrative Pronoun, *tōd, meaning 'from that,' 'thereupon.' Hence the use of this form for the 2d Sg. Fut. Imperat., e.g. Hor. C. iii. 14. 23:

> si per invisum mora janitorem
> fiet, abito,

abito, originally abi-tōd, meaning 'depart thereupon.'

louci must be Gen. of Possession, 'what belongs to the grove.' The Locative 'in the grove' (cf. humi, Corinthi) would at this early time be spelled loucei.

siet (Hist. Gram. vi. 13), a common form in Plautus, is almost an exact counterpart of the Greek εἴη, which represents an original ἐ(σ)ιη(τ). The Indo-European Optative Act. of Athematic Verbs shewed iē in the Sg., ī in the Plur. O. Latin siēs and sītis retain this old distinction; but in time the ī of the Plur. encroached on the Sg. too, and so in Class. Lat. sim, sis, sit replace siem, sies, siet.

nĕsei is the older form of nĭ-sī (nĭ-sĭ), in which the ĕ has become ĭ through Vowel-weakening in this unaccented word (§ 14), and ei has become ī. (Cf. p. 20 on noisi of the Dvenos inscription.)

res deina. Res divina, the common Latin phrase for a sacrifice, has this disyllabic form of the Adj. also in Plautus:

> quae dum rem dinam faceret cantaret mihi,

Republican Period. 55

a shortening due to the Latin tendency to pronounce *īvī* as *ī* (cf. *sis* for *si vis*). The form of the phrase on its recurrence in this inscription is interesting, **reidīnai**, for it indicates that *res divina* in pronunciation made one word like *respublica*, etc. See my *Hist. Gram.* ch. ii. § 11.

sei, class. *sī*, was originally a Locative Sg. of the Pronoun stem so- 'that,' lit. 'in that (case).' (*Hist. Gram.* ch. ix. § 13.) On the termination of **Iouē**, see § 8 (contrast **Iouei**, below).

bouīd. *Bov-* is really a Consonant-stem and not an I-stem, as we see from its Gen. Plur, *bo(v)-um* not *bovi-um*. But it here shews the I-stem Abl. ending *-īd* (§ 10). This form adds a fresh illustration of the confusion of Consonant and I-stems of the 3d Decl. (*Hist. Gram.* ch. iii. § 8. The Consonant-stems properly used for their Ablative the Locative Case, which ended in *-ĭ*, later *-ĕ*, so that we should expect to find here *bovĭ* or rather *bouĕ* (§ 21).

piaclum. The *-clum* of **piaclum** and similar words, originally *-tlŏm*, is a quite different termination from the Diminutive *-culus, -culum* of *puer-culus, mel-culum*, etc., which was originally *-cŏ-lŏs, -cŏ-lŏm*. But the tendency in pronunciation to facilitate the pronunciation of *-clum* by means of a parasitic vowel assimilated the two endings, so that Class. Lat. *piaculum* seems to have the same termination as a Diminutive like *mel-culum* (cf. *poplo-* No. 4, *pocolom* No. 5, and see my *Hist. Gram.* ch. ii. § 12; B. *App.* § 91).

scies. On the dropping of *n* before *s*, see § 22.

uiolasit. The O. Lat. Verb-forms in -*assim*, -*essim*, etc., e.g. *amassim*, *prohibessim*, are really Optatives of the same Tense of which forms in -*asso*, etc., e.g. *amasso*, are Subjunctives (with Future meaning, *Hist. Gram.* ch. vi. § 13). The Optative sense is the usual one with the forms in -*sim*. Thus *bene sponsis beneque volueris* was a formula of frequent use in the Augural prayer; another early prayer shews *Juppiter prohibessis scelus*, etc., etc. But they have also, as here, a conditional sense. In the classical language they were replaced in their Optative use by the Pres. Subj., and by the Perf. Subj. in their Conditional use. See my *Hist. Gram.* ch. vi. § 13.

dicatore (on this Dat. Sg. ending see § 8) may be a miswriting for *dictatore*. But it is possible that the Verb *dicare* (cf. *indicare*) had a Verbal Noun *dicator*.

Beside this we may put another inscription of the same purport, though more influenced by dialectal forms, and possibly of an earlier date: —

XXXIII. The Luceria Inscription, from Luceria in Apulia, on the borders of the Oscan Samnium. (*Eph. Epigr.* ii. 298.)

in hoce loucarid stircus nequis fundatid neue cadauer proiecitad neue parentatid. seiquis aruorsu hac faxit in ium quis uolet pro ioudicatod n. L. manum iniectio estod. seiue magisteratus uolet moltare licetod.

in hoc lucari (luco) stercus nequis fundet neve cadaver proiciat neve parentet. Siquis adversum hac fecerit, in

*eum quisquis volet projudicato. N(ummum) L manum
injectio esto. Sive magistratus volet multare, liceto.*

The curious Verb-forms **fundatid, proiecitad,** and **parentatid** are dialectal. They remind us of the Oscan forms with *t* or *tt* corresponding to Latin *ss*; so that **fundatid, parentatid** might be in genuine Latin *fundassit* and *parentassit,* while **proiecitad** might correspond to a suppositious *projecissat,* like *incipissat.* Dialectal, too, is the *i* of **stircus** and the parasitic vowel of **magisteratus** (cf. No. 15). Indications of the date of the inscription are **hoce** for *hocce* (originally *hōd-ce,* § 10), with single consonant written for double, **in** and **iniectio** with *ĕ* weakened to *ĭ*. Notice the omission of final *m* in **aruorsu(m),** and the spelling **ium** for *eum.* Points of grammar that require comment are (1) the Adverbial group **aruorsu(m) hac** with the Abl. Sg. Fem. of the Pronoun, like *praeter hac, praetereā,* etc. (cf. *aruorsum ead,* No. 37); (2) the Acc. **manum** governed by the Verbal Noun **iniectio,** like Plautus' *quid tibi hanc tactio est?* 'what do you mean by touching this lady?' On the form *ar-* for *ad-* in **aruorsu(m)** see *Hist. Gram.* ch. ii. § 8.

XXXIV. Decree of Aemilius Paulus, found in Spain. (189 B.C.) (*C.I.L.* II. 5041.)

L. Aimilius L. f. inpeirator decreiuit utei quei Hastensium seruei in turri Lascutana habitarent leiberei essent agrum oppidumque quod ea tempestate posedisent item possidere habereque iousit dum poplus senatusque Romanus uellet. Act. in castreis a.d. xii K. Febr.

L. Aemilius L. f. imperator decrevit ŭti qui Hastensium servi in turri Lascutana habitarent liberi essent: agrum oppidumque quod ea tempestate possedissent item possidere habereque jussit dum populus senatusque Romanus vellet. Act(um) in castris a(nte) d(iem) xii K(alendas) Febr(uarias).

The discovery of this inscription upset Ritschl's theory that final -*d* after a long vowel was still pronounced in the time of Plautus. Relying on the fact that *d* in the Abl. Sg. and 3d Sg. Imperat. is unfailingly written throughout the Senatus Consultum de Bacchanalibus, a decree of 186 B.C., two years before the death of Plautus, Ritschl argued that the *d* must have been still pronounced in these forms in the language of Plautus' day, and that when an Abl. is followed by a word beginning with a vowel in a line of Plautus there was not necessarily hiatus. The discovery, however, of this decree of Aemilius Paulus, with its omission of Abl. -*d*, shews that the retention of the letter on the Senatorial Decree is a mere piece of conservative spelling. Since a change in spelling always lags behind a change in pronunciation, there is every reason to believe that in the ordinary everyday talk of Plautus' time Ablatives like *terra*, *puero*, or Imperatives like *esto*, *abito*, were pronounced without any final consonant.

The inscription is also interesting in exhibiting the incoming fashion of writing double a double consonant. We have, e.g. *posedisent* close to *possidere*. The curious *ei* of **inpeirator** and **decreiuit** seems to express the same

Republican Period.   59

sound, viz. close *e*. The old diphthong is still retained in **Aimilius** and **iousit** (on which see No. 37).

To the same year belongs an inscription of M. Fulvius Nobilior, the patron of the poet Ennius. (*C.I.L.* I. 534.)

XXXV. M. Fuluius M. f. Ser. n. cos. Aetolia cepit.

> *M. Fulvius M. f. Ser. n(epos) co(n)s(ul) ex Aetolia cepit.*

Here **Aetolia**, if it be the Abl. as *Hinnad* of No. 20 indicates, lacks the old final *d*, like *turri, Lascutana, ea* of the last inscription.

Two years later is a milestone with the name of M. Aemilius Lepidus, the projector of the Via Aemilia, found near Bologna; 187 B.C. (*C.I.L.* I. 535.)

XXXVI. M. Aemilius M. f. M. n. Lepidus cos.

CC⊥ · XIIX

> *M. Aemilius M. f. M. n(epos) Lepidus co(n)s(ul).*

CCLXVIII

The figures give the number of miles between Rome and Bononia (now Bologna). Notice the modern form of the diphthong *ai* in the name **Aemilius** (§ 16).

Other milestones from the Via Aemilia of the same date shew the same form of the name.

XXXVII. The Senatus Consultum de Bacchanalibus, 186 B.C. On a bronze tablet affixed to the wall of a temple in South Italy. (*C.I.L.* I. 196.)

Q. Marcius L. f. S. Postumius L. f. cos. senatum consoluerunt N. Octob. apud aedem Duelonai. Sc. arf. M. Claudi M. f. L. Valeri P. f. Q. Minuci C. f. De Bacanalibus quei foideratei esent ita exdeicendum censuere. Neiquis eorum Bacanal habuise uelet. Seiques esent quei sibei deicerent necesus ese Bacanal habere eeis utei ad pr. urbanum Romam uenirent deque eeis rebus ubei eorum verba audita esent utei senatus noster decerneret dum ne minus senatoribus C adesent quom ea res cosoleretur. Bacas uir nequis adiese uelet ceiuis Romanus neue nominus Latini neue socium quisquam nisei pr. urbanum adiesent isque de senatuos sententiad dum ne minus senatoribus C adesent quom ea res cosoleretur iousiset. Censuere. Sacerdos nequis uir eset. Magister neque uir neque mulier quisquam eset. Neue pecuniam quisquam eorum comoinem habuise uelet neue magistratum neue pro magistratud neque uirum neque mulierem quisquam fecise uelet. Neue post hac inter sed coniourase neue comuouise neue conspondise neue conpromesise uelet neue quisquam fidem inter sed dedise uelet. Sacra in oquoltod ne quisquam fecise uelet neue in poplicod neue in preiuatod neue exstrad urbem sacra quisquam fecise uelet nisei pr. urbanum adieset isque de senatuos sententiad dum ne minus senatoribus C adesent quom ea res cosoleretur iousiset. Censuere. Homines plous V oinuorsei uirei atque mulieres sacra ne quisquam fecise uelet neue inter ibei uirei plous duobus mulieribus plous tribus arfuise uelent nisei de pr. urbani senatuosque sententiad utei suprad scriptum est. Haice utei in couentionid exdeicatis ne minus trinum noundinum senatuosque sententiam utei scientes esetis. Eorum sententia ita fuit sei ques esent quei aruorsum ead fecisent quam suprad scriptum est eeis rem caputalem faciendam censuere. Atque utei hoce in tabolam ahenam inceideretis ita senatus aiquom censuit uteique eam figier ioubeatis ubei facilumed gnoscier potisit atque utei ea Bacanalia sei qua sunt exstrad quam sei quid ibei sacri est ita utei suprad scriptum est in diebus X quibus uobeis tabelai datai erunt faciatis utei dismota sient.

Q. Marcius L. f., S(purius) Postumius L. f. cons. senatum consuluerunt N(onis) Octob. apud aedem Bellonae. Sc(ribendo) adf(uerunt) M. Claudius M. f., L. Valerius P. f., Q. Minucius C. f. De Bacchanalibus qui foederati essent ita edicendum censuere. Nequis eorum Bacchanal habuisse vellet. Siqui essent qui sibi dicerent necesse esse Bacchanal habere, ei ŭti ad pr(aetorem) urbanum Romam venirent, deque eis rebus, ubi eorum verba audita essent, ŭti senatus noster decerneret, dum ne minus senatoribus C adessent quum ea res consuleretur. Bacchas vir nequis adiisse vellet civis Romanus, neve nominis Latini, neve sociorum quisquam, nisi pr(aetorem) urbanum adiissent, isque de senatus sententia, dum ne minus senatoribus C adessent quum ea res consuleretur, jussisset. Censuere. Sacerdos nequis vir esset. Magister neque vir neque mulier quaequam esset: neve pecuniam quisquam eorum communem habuisse vellet, neve magistratum, neve pro magistratu neque virum neque mulierem quisquam fecisse vellet. Neve posthac inter se conjurasse neve convovisse, neve conspondisse, neve compromisisse vellet, neve quisquam fidem inter se dedisse vellet. Sacra in occulto ne quisquam fecisse vellet, neve in publico, neve in privato, neve extra urbem sacra quisquam fecisse vellet, nisi pr(aetorem) urbanum adiisset, isque de senatus sententia, dum ne minus senatoribus C adessent quum ea res consuleretur, jussisset. Censuere. Homines plus V universi, viri atque mulieres, sacra ne quisquam fecisse vellet, neve interibi viri plus duobus, mulieribus plus tribus, adfuisse vellent, nisi de pr(aetoris) urbani senatusque sententia, ŭti supra scriptum est. Haec ŭti in contione edicatis ne minus trinum nundinum, senatusque sententiam ŭti scientes essetis. Eorum sententia ita fuit: siqui essent qui adversum eā fecissent, quam supra scriptum est, eis rem capitalem faciendam censuere. Atque ŭti hoc in tabulam ahenam incideretis: ita senatus aequum censuit; ŭtique eam figi jubeatis, ubi facillime nosci possit; atque uti ea Bacchanalia, siqua sunt, extra quam siquid ibi sacri est, in diebus X, quibus vobis tabellae datae erunt, faciatis ŭti dimota sint.

This is a copy of the 'senatus vetus auctoritas de Bacchanalibus' mentioned by Cicero (*Legg.* ii. 15, 37). Livy (xxxix. 14. 7; cf. 17. 4) tells us that in 186 B.C. the senate determined 'edici in urbe Roma et per totam Italiam edicta mitti, ne quis qui Bacchis initiatus esset coisse aut convenisse causa sacrorum velit neu quid talis rei divinae fecisse.' This inscription is two years earlier than the death of Plautus (184 B.C.), in whose comedies we have more than one allusion to the Bacchanalian orgies and the disfavour in which they were coming to be held by the government (e.g. *Aul.* 408, *Bacch.* 53, *Mil.* 858, 1016, *Cas.* 980, nam ecastor nunc Bacchae nullae ludunt). So that this precious record of antiquity transports us into the very time of Plautus and Ennius, and gives us a glimpse of the language as it was spoken, or at least written, at the beginning of the second century B.C. Being a formal state document, its forms will rather be those of a previous generation than the actual colloquial forms of the speech of the day (on final -*d* of Ablatives, etc., see § 19).

The older ŏ appears instead of the later ŭ in **consoluerunt, cosoleretur**, etc. Diphthongs remain in their earlier shape, e.g. **Duelonai, aiquom**, etc.; in particular, the distinction between diphthongal *ei* and simple *ī* is observed in **deicerent**, beside **uenirent**, etc. Double consonants, though doubtless pronounced double, are written single, the practice of writing them double being a reform of the poet Ennius (§ 17).

Duelonai, class. *Bellonae*. On *du-*, class. *b-* (cf. *duonus* and *bonus*, *duis* and *bis*), see my *Hist. Gram.* ch. x. § 13; B. *App.* § 104. 2 *c*; *duellum*, the precursor of *bellum*, was a disyllabic word, as it is in Plautus. Horace's *duëllum* (3 syll.) has been called a pseudo-archaism.

Bacanalibus, class. *Bacchanalibus*. The use of *h* with a mute to represent the Greek aspirates was not known till the close of the Republic.

quei, originally the unaccented form (§ 5), *quoi* being the accented. In **foideratei**, originally *foideratoi*, the difference between the accented and unaccented diphthong is exemplified.

neiquis. *Nei*, later *nī*, is the O. Lat. Prohibitive Particle, used by Virgil 'antiquitatis amans' in *A.* iii. 686 : ni teneant cursus.

Bacanal, class. *Bacchanal*. The final ĕ has already been dropped (§ 21), but the *a* of the last syllable probably still retained its long quantity (§ 18); cf. Plaut. *Aul.* 413 aperitur Bacchanál: adest.

uelet is class. *vellet;* not *velit*, which has I.-Eur. ĭ in the last syllable, and which would be written *uelit* on an inscription of this date.

ques. The distinction between the I-stem *qui-* (Interrog., Indef.) and the O-stem *quŏ-* (Relative) is retained in Class. Lat. in the Acc. Sg. Neut., *quid* (Interrog., Indef.) beside *quod* (Rel.), but in early Latin was kept up in other cases too, such as the Nom. Plur. Cato's *Origines* began with the words: siques homines sunt, quos delectat populi Romani gesta describere.

necesus is said to be a Neuter Noun like *opus, genus.* But its exact relation to the form *necesse* (used by Plautus), and indeed the precise composition of this latter form, are doubtful.

eeis. The Demonstrative Pronouns often added to the *-ei* (class. *-ī*) of their Nom. Plur. Masc. the *-s* which was the Plur. ending of Nouns. Plautus affects these forms when the Particle *-ce* is added, *hīs-ce, illīs-ce*, etc.; Virgil is said to have used the archaic *hīs* in *Ecl.* iii. 102:—

his certe, neque amor causa est, vix ossibus haerent.

cosoleretur. On the absence of *n* see § 22.

adiesent, class. *adiissent.* For *ii* we usually find *ie* in Latin, e.g. *societas, laniena*, beside *caritas, officina.* But the *e* of **conpromesise** below suggests that this *e* is a relic of the old use of *e* for the diphthong-sound *ei.*

Republican Period. 65

nominus. The I.-Eur. Gen. Sg. of Consonant (3d Decl.) Stems ended either in -ŏs, or -ĕs. The Greeks adopted the first ending, the Romans the second (§ 10), though in early Latin we find isolated relics of the other form, a form which may have been long in use in the plebeian speech.

socium. Gen. Pl. (§ 10).

senatuos. On this 4th Decl. Gen., see my *Latin Language*, ch. vi. § 21.

iousiset. Apparently the first syllable of the Perfect of *jubeo* contained a diphthong originally, so that Class. Lat. *jŭssi* has taken the place of a discarded *jūsi*. We even find a diphthong in the Present tense, in early Latin (see **ioubeatis**, below). This indicates that there may have been two rival stems, *iŭb-* and *ioub-*, to which the confusion of quantity has been due.

magister was both Masc. and Fem. in early Latin, like *puer;* cf. Naevius, *Bell. Pun.* ii. (a Saturnian line):—

prima incédit Céreris Prosérpina púer.

conpromesise, see above on **adiesent.**

oquoltod. The I.-Eur. root kel-, to hide, began with k, not q. The spelling here shews that *quo* and *co* had come to have the same sound in Latin, and so were interchanged. Similarly, the Prep. *cum* (I.-Eur. kŏm) is often written *quom* in early Latin (e.g. No. 45).

poplicod. This curious spelling *popl-* is usually referred to a confusion between *pūblicus* (from *pūbes,* long *u* and *b*) and *pŏpulus* (with short *o* and *p*).

extrad. These Adverbs in -$\bar{a}$ were originally Abl. Sg. Fem. (see my *Hist. Gram.* ch. vii. § 4), and so appear in early Latin inscriptions with a final -*d* (§ 19).

plous. One would expect *plois* (*Hist. Gram.* ch. iv. § 3). Some compare the ending of *min-us;* but *ou* is more probably a mere spelling of the sound $\bar{u}$ (§ 16).

oinuorsei is merely a way of writing *oinu-uorsei*, and was doubtless pronounced as a quadrisyllable. Before *v* the weakened vowel remains $\breve{u}$ and does not sink to $\breve{\imath}$ as in class. *uni-versi*. On *vo-* for class. *ve-*, see § 22.

arfuise, class. *adfuisse*. On the curious usage at this time of writing (and pronouncing) *r* for *d* before *f* and *v*, see my *Hist. Gram.* ch. ii. § 8. This peculiarity of Old Latin was preserved in the legal formula SCR · ARF., *scribendo arfuerunt*.

couentionid. *Contio* was originally *co(m)-uentio*, as *nuntius* was originally *noventius* (from *novus*). Why *contio* should have *o* and *nuntius* the vowel *u* is not clear. Possibly the *m* of *com-* made the difference. This is the I-stem Ablative ending -*īd*, quite different from the Consonant-stem Locative ending (used as Abl.) -*ĭ*, later -*ĕ* (§ 10).

noundinum, class. *nundinum*, a Gen. Plur. (cf. **socium,** above), which came to be used as Neut. Sg. *nundinum*, -*i*. It is derived from *novem* and *dĭn-*, a by-stem of *dies*, a day. On *ou* for earlier *ŏvĕ* cf. the remarks above on the vocalism of *contio* and *nuntius*.

scientes esetis. This use of the Pres. Part. with the Substantive Verb is found in Plautus too, e.g. *Poen.* 1038.

aruorsum. See on **arfuise,** above.

ead shews that in *praeter-ea, propter-ea*, etc., *ea* is an Abl. Sg. Fem. Cf. *praeter-hac, post-hac*, etc., and *aruorsu hac* (No. 33).

suprad. See on **exstrad**, above.

caputalem. The *u* has not sunk to *i* (cf. **oinuorsei**, above).

hoce, that is *hŏcce* (§ 17), from older *hŏd-ce* (§ 10).

facilumed, class. *facillime*. These Adverbs in -*ē* were originally Ablatives. Possibly the 2d Decl. had in very early times two Ablative endings (1) -*ōd*, used for Nouns and some Adverbs, e.g. *modo, cito*, etc.; (2) -*ēd*, reserved for Adverbs only.

potisit, i.e. *potis sit*. *Potis* Masc., Fem. (here Fem.), *pote* Neut., were originally distinct. In course of time the Neut. *pote* came to be used in all cases. Hence class. *potest* for *pote est*, used with all subjects, Masc., Fem., or Neut. Virgil employs *potis est*, e.g. *Aen.* xi. 148:—

at non Evandrum potis est vis ulla tenere.

tabelai, class. *tabellae* 'despatches.' *Tabulae* would be *tabolai* (cf. **tabolam**, above).

dismota, class. *dīmota* (§ 22).

sient, the old 3d Plur. Pres. Subj. (properly Optative) of *sum* (see No. 32).

XXXVIII. Dedicatory inscription of a Faliscan 'collegium coquorum.' (*C.I.L.* xi. 3078.)

Gonlegium quod est aciptum aetatei agedai,
Opiparum ad ueitam quolundam festosque dies,
Quei soueis argutieis opidque Uolgani

Gondecorant saipisume comuinia loidosque,
Ququei huc dederunt inperatoribus summeis,
Utei sesed lubentes beneiouent optantis.

Iouei Iunonei Mineruai Falesce quei in Sardinia sunt donum
dederunt. Magistreis L. Latrius K. f. C. Saluena Voltai
f. coiraueront.

Collegium quod est acceptum aetati agendae,
opiparum ad vitam colendam festosque dies,
qui suis argutiis opeque Vulcani
condecorant saepissime convivia ludosque,
coqui hoc dederunt imperatoribus summis (i.e. Jupiter, Juno, Minerva),
ut sese libentes bene juvent optantes.

Jovi Junoni Minervae Falisci qui in Sardinia sunt donum
dederunt. Magistri L. Latrius K(aesonis) f(ilius), C.
Salvenna Vultae f(ilius) curaverunt.

The spelling of this inscription is as faulty as the metre (Saturnian?); witness *g* for *c* in **gonlegium, gondecorant, Volgani**; also **aciptum** (for *-cept-*), **ququei** (for *coq-*), etc. Notice the double consonant in **summeis**, a doubling not found in **aciptum**, etc.

quolundam. The *q*-guttural of *colo* (for *quolo*) is seen in *inquilinus,* beside *incola.*

soueis. *Ou* was originally the vocalism of the accented, *u* of the unaccented, form of this Possessive (I.-Eur. s(w)ĕwo-). The same is true of *puer*, of which the older spelling *pover* occurs in a sentence in Iambic

Senarii designed for a schoolboy's copying lesson (*C.I.L.* III. p. 962):—

> senem seuerum semper esse condecet.
> bene debet esse pouero qui discet bene.

Similarly the *ov* of *novus* becomes *u* in the unaccented form of the word, e.g. *de-nuo* for *de novo*.

loidos (see § 16), cf. **coiraueront**, below.

huc is the unaccented form of *hoc* Acc. Sg. Neut. (for *hŏd-ce, § 10). This unaccented form came to be reserved for the Adverb 'hither' (O. Lat. *hoc, Hist. Gram.* vii. 5).

magistreis adds the ordinary Nom. Plur. ending -*s* to the already formed Plur. in -*ei* (class. -*i*) (see *eeis*, No. 37).

XXXIX. The Dedicatory Tablet of the Vertuleii, found at Sora. (*C.I.L.* I. 1175; x. 5708.)

> M. P. Vertuleieis C. f.
> Quod re sua difeidens asper afleicta
> Parens timens heic uouit, uoto hoc soluto.
> Decuma facta poloucta, leibereis lubentes
> Donu danunt Hercolei maxsume mereto;
> Semol te orant se uoti crebro condemnes.

> *M(arcus), P(ublius) Vertuleii C(ai) f(ilii),*
> *Quod re sua diffidens asper afflicta*
> *parens timens hīc vovit, voto hoc soluto,*
> *decima facta, pollucta, liberi libentes*
> *donum dant Herculi maxime merito;*
> *simul te orant se voti crebro condemnes.*

Vertuleieis. On this form of the Nom. Plur. see on *magistreis* (No. 38) and cf. **leibereis**, below.

asper, not *aspere*, seems to be on the stone. Cf. Virg. rebus non asper egenis.

heic. The Adv. *hīc* 'here' was originally the Locative Case of the Pronoun *hīc*, and was spelled with *ei*, as here. Similarly *illīc* 'there' was Loc. of *ille* (*illīc* Plaut.) and was spelled *illeic* (cf. Gk. ἐκεῖ).

poloucta. *Pollucere Herculi decimam* was the current phrase for offering a tithe to Hercules; cf. Plaut. *Stich.* 233:—

  ut decumam partem Herculi polluceam.

Varro *L.L.* vi. 54 id dicitur 'polluctum,' quod a porriciendo est fictum; quom enim ex mercibus libamenta projecta sunt Herculi in aram, tum polluctum est.

danunt. Third Plurals of this formation are a feature of Old Latin. Cf. Liv. Andr. *Odyssey:*—

  pártim érrant, nequínont Graéciam redíre

'they stray in companies, and cannot win back to Greece,' with *nequinont* for *nequeunt* (*Hist. Gram.* vi. 20).

uoti . . . condemnes. Cf. Virg. *voti reus* and *damnabis tu quoque votis*.

XL. Statue of L. Manlius Acidinus, found at Aquileia; c. 181 B.C. (*C.I.L.* I. 538.)

L. Manlius L. f. Acidinus triu uir Aquileiae coloniae deducundae.

L. Manlius L. f. Acidinus triumvir Aquileiae coloniae deducendae.

The other two commissioners were P. Cornelius Scipio Nasica and C. Flaminius (Livy xl. 34; cf. xxxix. 55).
deducundae. The Gerundive in *-undus* (originally *-om-do-*) existed side by side with the Gerundive in *-endus* (originally *-em-do-*) in early Latin, but was dropped in the classical period (see my *Hist. Gram.* ch. vi. § 18).

XLI. Inscription of Claudius Marcellus, found at Luna; 155 B.C. (*C.I.L.* I. 539.)

M. Claudius M. f. Marcelus consol iterum.

M. Claudius M. f. Marcellus consul iterum.

This inscription has a more ancient appearance than the preceding, owing to its retention of the old spellings **consol** (§ 14) and **Marcelus** (§ 17).

XLII. The Dedicatory Inscriptions of Mummius; c. 146 B.C. (*C.I.L.* I. 542 sqq.)

(a)   L. Mummi L. f. cos.
ductu auspicio imperioque eius
Achaia capta Corinto deleto
Romam redieit triumphans ob hasce res bene gestas
quod in bello uouerat hanc aedem et signu
Herculis Victoris imperator dedicat.

L. Mummius L. f. co(n)s(ul)
ductu auspicio imperioque ejus
Achaia capta Corintho deleto,
Romam rediit triumphans. Ob has res bene gestas
quod in bello voverat, hanc aedem et signum
Herculis Victoris imperator dedicat.

72   *Handbook of Latin Inscriptions.*

(b)   Sancte.
de decuma uictor tibei Lucius Mummius donum
moribus antiqueis promiserat hoc dare sese
uisum animo suo perfecit tua pace rogans te
cogendei dissoluendei tu ut facilia faxseis
perficias decumam ut faciat uerae rationis
proque hoc atque alieis doneis des digna merenti.

                        · *Sancte.*
de decima victor tibi Lucius Mummius donum
moribus antiquis promiserat hoc dare sese.
Visum animo suo perfecit, tua pace rogans te
cogendi dissolvendi tu ut facilia faxis (i.e. *facias*).
Perficias decimum ut faciat verae rationis;
proque hoc atque aliis donis des digna merenti.

Mummius, the conqueror of Corinth and Carthage, offered tithes of his booty to Hercules Victor (see on No. 39). These two inscriptions are dedicatory verses accompanying the gifts. It is possible that they are not the actual lines of Mummius, but a later copy, made when the inscription was renewed; for the presence of *ch* in **Achaia**, *ph* in **triumphans** (but *t* in **Corinto**), at so early a period is strange.

(a) **Mummi(s)**. On this form of the Nom. Sg. of IO-stems, see on *Minuci*, No. 19.

ductu auspicio imperioque. This was a current phrase. Cf. Plaut. *Amph.* 196:—

           ductu imperio auspicio suo.

Corinto, Masc. or Neut.?

redieit. The retention of the diphthong implying long

quantity of the final syllable may be due to the precedence of *i*, just as *diēi* retains long *e*, shortened in *fĭdĕi*. Even Ovid scans *rediīt*, etc. (but cf. *petiei*, No. 46).

hasce. The metre (Saturnian) seems to require monosyllabic pronunciation, *hasc*. (See § 13.)

On **signu(m)** see § 20. The last line of the inscription may be an Iambic Senarius.

(*b*) **promiserat.** The word is doubtful, for the inscription is now lost. The vulgar reading is *pro usura*.

suo, a monosyllable, as in Lucretius i. 1022, v. 420.

tua pace, Abl. like Plaut. *Rud.* 268 : —

fac ut ulciscare nosque ut hanc tua pace aram obsidere Patiare.

The Accusative Case is out of the question, for a scansion like *pacĕm rogans* would be impossible, even in such rude lines as these.

cogendei dissoluendi, etc. "that you would smooth the path for him in amassing and spending."

facilia, to make a dactyl, must be pronounced *faclia*, like *balneum* for *balineun* (see § 3).

On *faxis* see p. 56. *Xs* is a common spelling at this period for *x* (see below on *saxsum*, No. 45).

(*B*) FROM THE GRACCHI TO SULLA.

In this period the doubling of long vowels is found. For *ī* either *ei* or *I* is written.

XLIII. Inscription of Atilius Sarranus, found in North Italy; 135 B.C. (*C.I.L.* I. 549.)

Sex. Atilius M. f. Saranus procos. ex senati consulto inter
Atestinos et Veicetinos finis terminosque statui iusit.

Sex. Atilius M. f. Sarranus proco(n)s(ul) ex senatus consulto inter Atestinos et Vicentinos finis terminosque statui jussit.

Double consonants are still written single on this stone,
e.g. **Saranus**.

senati is not an unusual Genitive. Quintilian declared
it to be in his time as good a form as *senatūs* (see my
Hist. Gram. p. 58; B. *App.* § 162).

XLIV. Milestone of Popillius, found in Lucania; 132
B.C. (*C.I.L.* I. 551.)

uiam fecei ab Regio ad Capuam et in ea uia ponteis omneis
miliarios tabelariosque poseiuei hince sunt Nouceriam meilia
⊥I Capuam XXCIIII Muranum ⊥XXIIII Cosentiam CXXIII
Ualentiam C⊥XXX ad fretum ad statuam CCXXXI Regium
CCXXXVII suma af Capua Regium meilia CCCXXI et eidem
praetor in Sicilia fugiteiuos Italicorum conquaeisiuei redideique
homines DCCCCXVII eidemque primus fecei ut de agro poplico
aratoribus cederent paastores forum aedisque poplicas heic fecei.

*viam feci ab Rhegio ad Capuam et in ea via pontes
omnes miliarios tabellariosque posui. Hinc sunt Nuceriam
milia LI, Capuam LXXXIV, Muranum LXXIV, Consentiam
CXXIII, Valentiam CLXXX, ad fretum ad statuam CCXXXI,
Rhegium CCXXXVII; summa ab Capua Rhegium milia
CCCXXI. Et idem praetor in Sicilia fugitivos Italicorum
conquisivi, reddidique homines DCCCCXVII; idemque primus feci ut de agro publico aratoribus cederent pastores;
forum aedisque publicas hic feci.*

By this time *ī* and *ei* express the same sound, and the diphthong is merely used to express the long sound of the simple vowel; e.g. **ponteis omneis** were at no period pronounced with the diphthong *ei* (§ 16). Double consonants are written single throughout the inscription, e.g.

tabelarios, suma, redidei.

Regio. The spelling *rh* for Greek ρ did not come in till the end of the Republic.

poseiuei. The form *posui*, a form due to false analogy, has not yet ousted the true form *po-sīvi*. *Pono*, for **po-s(i)no*, is a compound of the old Prep. *pŏ* (Gk. ἀπό) and *sino*, and properly formed its Perfect *po-sivi* as its Supine *po-sĭtum*. But the analogy of *monĭtum*, etc., suggested that a Supine *positum* should have a Perfect *posui;* and this erroneous form gradually ousted the other, which, however, is exclusively used by the older writers. (See my *Hist. Gram.* ch. xi. § 21; B. *App.* § 261. 4.)

meilia. The word was at this time pronounced with double *l*; but on this inscription double consonants are written single. About the time of Augustus *ll* between *ī* and *i* was reduced to *l*. Hence *mīlia*, older *mīllia; vīlicus*, older *vīllicus*, etc. See my *Hist. Gram.* ch. ii. § 9.

Cosentiam, see § 22.

af. The origin of this by-form of *a, ab* is uncertain. See my *Hist. Gram.* ch. vii. § 2.

eidem. The *ei* expresses the sound *ī* of *īdem* (for *is-dem*, § 22).

conquaeisivei. The *aei* is a curious spelling, half-way between *ai* and *ei*.

poplico, see on *poplicod*, No. 37.

paastores. This method of indicating a long vowel, by doubling it, just as a long consonant was written double, was introduced by the poet Accius, and gained favour for a time. Afterwards it was discarded for the "apex," an accent-sign placed above the vowel to indicate the length, e.g. PÁSTORES. See § 17.

heic. This is the original spelling of the Adverb *hīc*, properly the Locative Case of the Pronoun; see on *heic*, No. 39.

XLV. Epitaph of a Scipio, in Saturnian metre. (*C.I.L.* I. 34; VI. 1289.)

L. Cornelius Cn. f. Cn. n. Scipio.
magna sapientia multasque uirtutes
aetate quom parua posidet hoc saxsum
quoiei Vita defecit non Honos honore
is hic situs quei nunquam uictus est uirtutei
annos gnatus XX is loceis mandatus
ne quairatis honore quei minus sit mandatus.

L. Cornelius Cn. f. Cn. n(epos) Scipio.
Magnam sapientiam multasque virtutes
aetate cum parva possidet hoc saxum.
Cui Vita defecit non Honos honorem,
is hic situs, qui nunquam victus est virtute.
Annos natus viginti is (? iis) locis mandatus.
Ne quaeratis honorem qui minus sit mandatus.

quom. Since *quo* had come to be pronounced like *co* the two are often interchanged (see on *oquoltod*, No. 37).

posidet. The double consonant is written single in this word, but double in **annos,** below.

saxsum. *Xs* is a common way of writing *x* in early inscriptions, and indeed in Latin of all periods (cf. *exstrad* No. 37, *faxseis* No. 42, *saxso* No. 66 (5), etc.).

quoiei. On this form see § 10. The Relative in Latin formed its Gen. and Dat. by adding to its Instrumental Case *quō* the Gen. and Dat. of the Demonstr. Pron. **quō-eios,** *quō-eiei* (*Hist. Gram.* ch. v. § 6).

honore(m) (so below), Acc. after **defecit** 'stinted.' On the absence of *-m* see § 20.

virtutei, i.e. *virtutī* (§ 17), is the I-stem Abl. (originally *-tīd*, § 10), while the classical form *virtutĕ* (originally *virtutī*, § 21) is really the Loc. (§ 10).

hic is the Adv. *hīc*.

is is naturally taken as Nom. Sg. 'he.' It may also be Dat. Plur. agreeing with **loceis** 'assigned to this grave' (cf. *loculus*); for the use of *is*, where *hic* would be the proper Pron., is not unknown in writers of this time. The reading **loceis** is due to conjecture, there being a gap in the stone. Buecheler prefers **diueis** (i.e. the Manes).

quairatis. The old spelling is retained, though the diphthong was now certainly pronounced *ae*.

quei is Adverbial *quī* 'how': 'do not ask how it was that honour was not assigned to him,' lit. 'do not ask about honour how it was,' etc. This is the common Latin idiom, e.g. *novi te qualis sis*, like the Gk. οἶδά σε ὅστις εἶ.

Another rendering is 'do not ask about his honours, for they (lit. 'which') were never granted him.'

XLVI. Epitaph of Cn. Cornelius Scipio Hispanus, in Elegiac metre; praetor 139 B.C. (*C.I.L.* I. 38; VI. 1293.)

Cn. Cornelius Cn. f. Scipio Hispanus pr. aid. cur. q. tr. mil. II Xuir sl. iudik. Xuir sacr. fac.

uirtutes generis mieis moribus accumulaui
progenie mi genui facta patris petiei
maiorum optenui laudem ut sibei me esse creatum
laetentur stirpem nobilitauit honor.

Cn. Cornelius Cn. f. Scipio Hispanus pr(aetor), aed(ilis) cur(ulis), q(uaestor), tr(ibunus) mil(itaris), bis decemvir l(itibus) judic(andis), decemvir sacr(is) fac(iendis).

virtutes generis meis moribus accumulavi,
progeniem mi genui, facta patris petii,
majorum obtinui laudem, ut sibi me esse creatum
laetentur; stirpem nobilitavit honor.

sl. On *stlis*, *slis*, old forms of *lis*, see *Hist. Gram.* ch. x. § 19; B. *App.* § 104. 1 *d*. Notice the *k* of **iudik(andeis)**.

mieis, monosyllabic, like *suo* (No. 42 *b*). On the spelling with *i*, which avoided the awkward form *meeis* (mistakable for *mēis*), see my *Latin Language*, ch. ii. § 9.

progenie(m). On the dropping of *-m* see § 20. This word must be pronounced apparently *prōgĕnyĕ* (? *prŏgĕnĭĕ*, like *făcĭlĭă*, No. 42 *b*) to suit the metre. Buecheler prefers to read *progeniem genui*.

petiei. The *ei* of **petiei** beside the *i* of **accumulaui** is due

Republican Period. 79

to the desire to avoid the spelling *ii* which might represent *ji* or even *ī* (cf. *paastores* in No. 44).

optenui. *Op* represents the sound actually pronounced, as we know from Quintilian (i. 7. 7).

sibei. The metre requires *sibĭ*, but the old spelling is retained. Cf. *tibei* No. 42 *b*.

nobilitauit. By this time a long vowel had become shortened before a final *t* (see § 18).

XLVII. Epitaph in Iambic senarii found at Rome; of the time of the Gracchi. (*C.I.L.* I. 1007; VI. 15346.)

> hospes, quod deico, paullum est, asta ac pellege.
> heic est sepulcrum hau pulcrum pulcrai feminae.
> nomen parentes nominarunt Claudiam.
> suom mareitum corde deilexit souo.
> gnatos duos creauit, horunc alterum
> in terra linquit, alium sub terra locat.
> sermone lepido, tum autem incessu commodo.
> domum seruauit; lanam fecit. dixi. abei.

Sepulcrum (from *sĕpelio*) was vulgarly derived from *sē* 'without' and *pulcher* 'beautiful.'

Commodus in the early literature often means 'graceful' 'correct,' (*-cum modo*) e.g. Plaut. *Most.* 254–5:—

PH. suo quisque loco (uiden?) capillus satis compositust
   commode?
SC. ubi tu commoda es, capillum commodum esse credito.

Lanifica is a commendatory epithet in epitaphs on Roman ladies.

Ei is used on this inscription not only for the older diphthong (as in **deico, heic, abei**), but also for a long simple *i* as in **deilexit** (cf. § 16). Another mixture of old and new spelling is **pulcrai** (a disyllable) beside **feminae**.

paullum would be *paulum* in the classical spelling (*Hist. Gram.* ii. 9).

Souo- is the older spelling, while *suo-* was originally proper to the unaccented use of the word (cf. *nóvus* beside *dénuo;* see on *soueis*, No. 38).

Hau was the proper form before an initial consonant, *haud* before an initial vowel (§ 19).

XLVIII. The Law of Bantia. On a bronze tablet, which contained on the other side a law in the Oscan language, found at Bantia in Lucania; 133–118 B.C. (*C.I.L.* I. 197.)

... deicito neiue quis mag. testumonium poplice ei ... Neiue is in poplico luuci praetextam neiue soleas. ... Mag. queiquomque comitia conciliumue habebit eum sufragium ferre nei sinito ... quei ex hace lege plebeiue scito factus erit senatorue fecerit gesseritue quo ex hace lege ... ex h. l. facere oportuerit oportebitue non fecerit sciens d. m. seiue aduorsus hance legem fecerit ... eam pequniam quei uolet magistratus exsigito. Sei postulabit quei petet pr. recuperatores ... oporteat dato iubetoque eum sei ita pariat condumnari populo facitoque ioudicetur. Sei condemnatus ... ad q. urb. det aut bona eius poplice possideantur facito. Seiquis mag. multam inrogare uolet ... partus familias taxsat liceto eiq. omnium rerum siremps lexs esto quasei sei

Republican Period. 81

is haace lege ... nunc est is in diebus V proxsumeis quibus queique eorum sciet h. l. popolum plebemue ... eis in diebus V proxsumeis quibus quisque eorum mag. inperiumve inierit iouranto. ... Castorus palam luci in forum uorsus et eidem in diebus V apud q. iouranto per Iouem deosque ... facturum neque sese aduorsum h. l. facturum scientem d. m. neque seese facturum neque intercesurum. ... Quei ex h. l. non iourauerit is magistratum inperiumue nei petito neiue gerito neiue habeto neiue in senatu ... ni quis sinito neiue eum censor in senatum legito ...

(neve is testimonium) dicito neve quis mag(istratus) testimonium publice ei (deferri neve denuntiari sinito). ... Neve is in publico luce praetextam neve soleas (habeto). ... Mag(istratus) quicumque comitia conciliumve habebit eum suffragium ferre ne sinito ... (Si judex) qui ex hac lege plebive scito factus erit, senatorve fecerit gesseritve, quo ex hac lege (quae fieri oporteat minus fiant quaeve) ex h(ac) l(ege) facere oportuerit oportebitve non fecerit sciens d(olo) m(alo); sive adversus hanc legem fecerit (. . . multa . . . esto et) eam pecuniam qui volet magistratus exigito. Si postulabit qui petet, pr(aetor) recuperatores ... (quos quotque dari) oporteat dato jubetoque eum, si ita pariat, condemnari populo facitoque judicetur. Si condemnatus (erit, quanti condemnatus erit, praedes) ad q(uaestorem) urb(anum) det aut bona ejus publice possideantur facito. Siquis mag(istratus) multam irrogare volet (qui volet, dum minoris) partis familiae taxat, liceto eiq(ue) omnium rerum siremps lex esto, quasi si is hac lege (pecuniam quae supra scripta est exegisset. Consul . . .) qui nunc est, is in diebus V proximis, quibus quique eorum sciet h(anc) l(egem) popu-

lum plebemve (jussisse, juranto ŭti infra scriptum est. Item dictator, consul . . . quicumque eorum post hac factus erit), ei in diebus V proximis, quibus quisque eorum mag(istratum) inperiumve inierit, juranto (ŭti infra scriptum est. Ei consistunto ante aedem) Castoris palam luce in forum versus et eidem in diebus V apud q(uaestorem) juranto per Jovem deosque (Penates sese quae ex hac lege oportebit) facturum, neque sese adversum h(anc) l(egem) facturum scientem d(olo) m(alo), neque sese facturum neque intercessurum (quo quae ex hac lege oportebit minus fiant). Qui ex hac lege non juraverit, is magistratum imperiumve ne petito neve gerito neve habeto neve in senatu (sententiam dicito dicereve eum) nequis sinito neve eum censor in senatum legito. . . .

neiue. See on *neiquis*, No. 37.

poplice. See on *poplicod*, No. 37.

pequniam. The spelling *qu* for *quu (quo)* was in vogue about this time.

pariat, probably a mere misspelling of *pareat*.

condumnari. Before a labial in the earlier literary period a reduced vowel often sinks to *ŭ*, not *ĕ (ĭ)*; see on *oinuorsei*, No. 37. Cf. **testumonium,** above.

partus. For this Gen. ending see on *nominus*, No. 37. Cf. **Castorus,** below.

taxsat. *Taxat,* Pres. Subj. of *taxo (for *tag-so), a by-form of *tango,* as *viso* of *video,* was retained in the legal phrase *dum taxat,* which in Classical Latin has become a mere Conj. *dumtaxat* (see my *Latin Language,* ch. ix. § 7). On *xs* for *x*, a prevalent spelling on this inscription, see on *saxsum,* No. 45.

siremps. This is a mysterious word which puzzled the Latin Grammarians. It occurs in the prologue of the *Amphitruo* of Plautus (v. 73):—

> sirempse legem iussit esse Iuppiter,

and in old laws it is fairly common in this formula: *siremps lex esto* 'the same law shall hold' (see my *Latin Language*, ch. ix. § 8).

XLIX. The Aletrium Temple inscription, on the front of a temple at Aletrium in Latium. (*C.I.L.* I. 1166.)

L. Betilienus L. f. Vaarus haec quae infera scripta sont de senatus sententia facienda coirauit semitas in oppido omnis, porticum qua inarcem eitur campum ubei ludunt horologium macelum basilicam calecandam seedes lacum balinearium lacum ad portam aquam in opidum adque arduom pedes CCCX↓ fornicesque fecit fistulas soledas fecit. Ob hasce res censorem fecere bis senatus filio stipendia mereta ese iousit populusque statuam donauit Censorino.

L. Betilienus L. f(ilius) Varus haec quae infra scripta sunt de senatus sententia facienda curavit: semitas in oppido omnis, porticum qua in arcem itur, campum ubi ludunt, horologium, macellum, basilicam calcandam, sedes, lacum balnearium, lacum ad portam, aquam in oppidum adque (atque?) arduum pedes CCCXL, *fornicesque fecit, fistulas soledas fecit. Ob hasce res censorem fecere bis, senatus filio stipendia merita esse jussit, populusque statuam donavit Censorino.*

infera, class. *infra;* cf. *supera*, No. 54 *a*.

inarcem. The Prep. and Noun were often written together, as they were always pronounced together (*Hist. Gram.* ii. 11). Cf. Nos. 59, 60.

calecandam. Lat. *calx*, lime, is a loan-word from the Gk. (χάλιξ), and was originally a disyllable.

balinearium. On *balinĕum* (Gk. βαλανεῖον) (cf. *platĕa* from Gk. πλατεῖα), see § 12.

in opidum adque arduom. Here we seem to have the original meaning of oppidum 'the town on the plain' as opposed to 'the fortress on the hill.' The word is the same as Gk. πέδον, ground, ἐπίπεδος, flat. So the Adv. *oppido* is like *plane*.

iousit. On the diphthong see *iousiset*, No. 37.

L. The Lex Repetundarum, on bronze tablets, found at Rome, 123–122 B.C. (*C.I.L.* I. 198.) (Extract.)

. . . De nomine deferundo iudicibusque legundeis. Quei ex h. l. pequniam ab . . . eum annum lectei erunt ad iudicem, in eum annum quei ex h. l. factus erit inious educito nomenque eius deferto. Sei deiurauerit calumniae causa non . . . erit de CDL uireis quei in eum annum ex h. l. lectei erunt aruorsario edat eos omnes . . . priuignusue siet queiue ei sobrinus siet propiusue eum ea cognatione attingat queiue ei sodalis siet queiue in eodem conlegio siet. Facitoque coram aruorsario . . . non attingeret scientem d. m. itaque is edito iouratoque. Ubei is ita ediderit, tum in eam . . . erit facito utei is die uicensumo ex eo die quo quoiusque quisque nomen detolerit Ouiros ex eis quei ex h. l. CDL uirei in eum annum lectei erunt quei uiuat legat . . . siet quoi is queiue ei quei petet gener socer uitricus priuignusque siet queiue ei sobrinus . . . ei sodalis siet queiue

Republican Period. 85

tr. pl. q. III uir cap. III uir a. d. a. tribunus mil. l. IIII primis
aliqua earum siet fueritue queiue insenatu siet fueritue queiue
l. Rubria . . . aberit queiue trans mare erit neiue amplius de
una familia unum neiue eum . . . Oalpurnia aut lege Iunia
sacramento actum siet aut quod h. l. nomen delatum siet. Quos
is Ouiros ex h. l. ediderit de eis ita facito iouret palam apud se
coram . . . necesitudine atingat quae supra scripta sient. Is
unde petitum erit quominus. . . . Ouiros ediderit iuraritue.
Tum eis pr. facito utei is unde petetur die LX postquam eius
nomen delatum erit quos O is quei petet ex h. l. ediderit de eis
iudices quos . . . nomen ex h. l. delatum erit L iudices ex h. l.
non legerit edideritue seiue . . . sodalitate atingat queiue in
eodem conlegio siet ex h. l. non . . . eum pr. aduorsariumue
mora non erit quo minus legat edatue . . . ioudicem legat.
Quei ita lectei erunt eis in eam rem ioudices sunto eorumque eius
. . . utei scripta in taboleis habeantur. Pr. quei ex h. l. quaeret
facito . . . quos is quei petet et unde petetur ex h. l. legerint
ediderint eosque patronos . . . quei petiuerit et unde petitum
erit quei eorum nolet extaboleis poplicis . . . Eisdem ioudices
unius rei in perpetuom sient. Quei iudices . . . quam in rem
eis iudices lectei erunt . . . quei pequniam ex h. l. capiet eum
ob eam rem quod pequniam ex h. l. ceperit . . . moueto neiue
equom adimito neiue quid ob eam rem fraudei esto. . . .

*. . . De nomine deferendo judicibusque legendis. Qui
ex h(ac) l(ege) pecuniam ab ⟨altero petet, is eum unde petet
. . . postquam* **CDL** *viri ex hac lege in⟩ cum annum lecti
erunt, ad judicem, in eum annum qui ex h(ac) l(ege) factus
erit, in jus educito nomenque ejus deferto. Si dejeraverit
calumniae causa non ⟨postulare, is praetor nomen recipito
itaque facito . . . ut die . . . ex eo die, quo cujusque quisque*

nomen detulerit, is cujus nomen delatum⟩ erit de CDL *viris qui in eum annum ex h(ac) l(ege) lecti erunt, adversario edat eos omnes ⟨ . . . cui is quive ei cujus nomen delatum erit gener socer vitricus⟩ privignusve sit quive ei sobrinus sit propiusve eum ea cognatione attingat, quive ei sodalis sit, quive in eodem collegio sit. Facitoque coram adversario ⟨is cujus nomen delatum erit juret, de* CDL *viris, qui in eum annum ex hac lege lecti sint, praeterea nullum esse nisi qui se earum aliqua neçessitudine, quae supra scripta sint⟩ non attingeret scientem d(olo) m(alo) itaque is edito juratoque. Ubi is ita ediderit, tum in eam ⟨quaestionem qui cujusque ita nomen detulerit, praetor, cujus ex hac lege quaestio⟩ erit, facito uti is die vicesimo ex eo die quo cujusque quisque nomen detulerit Cviros ex eis qui ex h(ac) l(ege)* CDL *viri in eum annum lecti erunt qui vivat legat ⟨edatque . . . dum nequis judex⟩ sit cui is quive ei qui petet gener socer vitricus privignusque sit quive ei sobrinus ⟨sit propiusve eum ea cognatione attingat, quive in eodem collegio sit, quive⟩ ei sodalis sit quive tr(ibunus) pl(ebis), q(uaestor), III vir cap(italis), III vir a(gris) d(andis) a(ssignandis), tribunus mil(itum) l(egionibus) IIII primis aliqua earum sit fueritve, quive in senatu sit fueritve, quive l(ege) Rubria ⟨III vir coloniae deducendae creatus sit fueritve, . . . quive ab urbe Roma plus . . milia passuum⟩ aberit, quive trans mare erit; neve amplius de una familia unum, neve eum ⟨legat edatve, qui pecuniae captae condemnatus est erit aut quod cum eo lege⟩ Calpurnia aut lege Junia sacramento actum sit aut quod h(ac) l(ege) nomen delatum sit. Quos is Cviros ex h(ac) l(ege) ediderit, de eis ita facito juret palam apud se coram ⟨adversario eorum nullum* se edidisse scientem dolo malo, quem ob earum causarum aliquam de ea re judicare non liceat quive se earum aliqua⟩ necessitudine attingat, quae supra scripta sint. Is unde petitum erit quominus ⟨ex hac lege ex reis eximatur, per eum praetorem adversariumque mora non erit, nisi is qui petet ita C⟩ viros ediderit juraritque. Tum eis pr(aetor) facito ut is unde petetur die LX postquam ejus nomen delatum erit, quos C is qui petet ex h(ac) l(ege) ediderit de eis judices quos ⟨volet L legat . . . Qui ex hac lege nomen detulerit, si is, cujus⟩ nomen ex h(ac) l(ege) delatum erit, L judices ex h(ac) l(ege) non legerit ediderítve, sive ⟨ex CDL viris qui in eum annum ex hac lege lecti erunt qui se affinitate cognatione⟩ sodalitate attingat, quive in eodem collegio sit ex h(ac) l(ege) non ⟨ediderit, tum ei per⟩ eum pr(aetorem) adversariumve mora non erit quominus legat edatve ⟨quos volet L de eis C quos ex hac lege ediderit . . . dum nequem eorum, quem ex hac lege de ea re judicare non liceat, sciens dolo malo⟩ judicem legat. Qui ita lecti erunt ei in eam rem judices sunto, eorumque ejus ⟨rei ex hac lege judicatio litisque aestimatio esto. Judicum patronorumque nomina⟩ ut scripta in tabulis habeantur. Pr(aetor) qui ex h(ac) l(ege) quaeret facito ⟨eos L viros⟩ quos is qui petet et unde petetur ex h(ac) l(ege) legerint ediderint eosque patronos, ⟨quos ei qui petet ex hac lege dederit . . . in tabulis publicis scriptos in perpetuo habeat. Ea nomina⟩ qui petierit et unde petitum erit qui eorum uolet ex tabulis publicis ⟨describere, is praetor permittito potestatemque scribendi facito⟩. Idem judices unius rei in perpetuum sint. Qui judices ⟨ex hac lege lecti erunt,⟩ quam in rem ei judices lecti erunt, ⟨ejus rei judices *in perpetuum sunto . . . ⟩ qui pecuniam ex h(ac) l(ege) capiet, eum ob eam rem quod pecuniam ex h(ac) l(ege) ceperit ⟨ne . . neve tribu⟩ moveto neve equum adimito neve quid ob eam rem fraudi esto.*

Notice the frequent writing of the Preposition in the same word with its Noun (e.g. **inious** 'injus,' **insenatu**), the spelling *qu* for *cu* (*quu*) (e.g. **pequniam**), the occasional use of a single for a double consonant (**necesitudine atingat**), the retention (not, however, consistently) of the old diphthongs (e.g. **ious, iourato**), and of *ŏ* for *ŭ* (e.g. **detolerit**), the Nom. Plur. of the Demonstrative in -(*e*)*is*, e.g. **eis eis-dem**. Of the Relative the forms in use are Nom. *quei*, Gen. *quoius*, Dat. *quoi* (see § 10). The Prohibitive Particle is *nei* (*nī*), on which see *neiquis*, No. 37.

LI. Inscriptions of magistrates of Capua.

(*a*) 108 B.C. (*C.I.L.* I. 565.)

. . . Heisce magistreis Venerus Iouiae murum aedificandum coirauerunt ped. CC⊥XX et loidos fecerunt Ser. Sulpicio M. Aurelio cos.

(*b*) 106 B.C. (*C.I.L.* I. 566.)

. . . Heisce magistreis Cererus murum et pluteum long. p. ⊥XXX alt. p. XXI faciund. coirauere eidemque loid. fec. O. Atilio Q. Seruilio cos.

(*c*) 106 B.C. (*C.I.L.* I. 567.)

. . . Heisce magistrei Castori et Polluci murum et pluteum faciund. coerauere eidemque loedos fecere Q. Seruilio C. Atilio cos.

Republican Period.

(a) *Hi magistri Veneris Joviae murum aedificandum curaverunt ped(es) CCLXX et ludos fecerunt Ser. Sulpicio M. Aurelio cos.*

(b) *Hi magistri Cereris murum et pluteum long(os) pedes LXXX alt(os) p(edes) XXI faciund(os) curavere idemque lud(os) fec(ere) C. Atilio Q. Servilio cos.*

(c) *Hi magistri Castori et Polluci murum et pluteum faciend(os) curavere idemque ludos fecere Q. Servilio C. Atilio cos.*

Notice the Nom. Plur. in -*eis* not merely of pronouns (see on *eeis* No. 37, *eis* No. 50), but also of nouns, e.g. **magistreis**; and the Gen. Sg. in -*us* (**Venerus, Cererus**), see on *nominus*, No. 37.

On **Venerus Iouiae** see *Ioues*, No. 2.

LII. Decree of the Pagus Herculaneus, 94 B.C. (*C.I.L.* I. 571.)

Pagus Herculaneus sciuit a. d. X Terminalia.

Conlegium seiue magistrei Iouei compagei sunt utei in porticum paganam reficiendam pequniam consumerent ex lege pagana arbitratu Cn. Laetori Cn. f. magistrei pagei uteique ei conlegio seiue magistri sunt Iouei compagei locus in teatro esset tam quasei sei ludos fecissent. . . . C. Coelio C. f. Caldo, L. Domitio Cn. f. Ahenobarbo cos.

Pagus Herculaneus scivit a(nte) d(iem) X Terminalia.

Collegium, sive magistri Jovii compagi sunt, ut in porticum paganam reficiendam pecuniam consumerent ex lege pagana arbitratu Cn. Laetorii Cn. f. magistri pagi; utque ei collegio, sive magistri sunt Jovii compagi, locus in theatro

*esset tam quasi si ludos fecissent . . . C. Coelio C. f(ilio),
L. Domitio Cn. f(ilio) Ahenobarbo cos.*

pequniam. For this spelling cf. No. 51.

teatro. The use of *th* for Gk. θ had not yet come in (§ 23).

LIII. Lex Cornelia de XX Quaestoribus, on a bronze tablet found at Rome; 81 B.C. (*C.I.L.* I. 202.)

. . . Cos. quei nunc sunt, iei ante k. Decembreis primas de eis, quei ciues Romanei sunt, uiatorem unum legunto, quei in ea decuria uiator appareat, quam decuriam uiatorum ex noneis Decembribus primeis quaestoribus ad aerarium apparere oportet oportebit. Eidemque cos. ante k. Decembr. primas de eis, quei ciues Romanei sunt, praeconem unum legunto, quei in ea decuria praeco appareat, quam decuriam praeconum ex noneis Decembribus primeis quaestoribus ad aerarium apparere oportet oportebit. . . . Eosque uiatores eosque praecones omneis, quos eo ordine dignos arbitrabuntur, legunto. Quam in quisque decuriam ita uiator lectus erit, is in ea decuria uiator esto item utei ceterei eius decuriae uiatores erunt. Quamque in quisque decuriam ita praeco lectus erit, is in ea decuria praeco esto ita utei ceterei eius decuriae praecones erunt. Sirempsque eis uiatoribus deque eis uiatoribus q(uaestori) omnium rerum iuus lexque esto, quasei sei uiatores in eam decuriam in tribus uiatoribus antea lectei sublectei essent. Sirempsque eis praeconibus deque eis praeconibus quaestori omnium rerum iuus lexque esto, quasei sei ei praecones in eam decuriam in tribus praeconibus antea lectei sublectei essent, quam in quisque decuriam eorum ex hac lege praeco lectus erit.

Quos quomque quaestores ex lege plebeiue scito uiatores legere sublegere oportebit, ei quaestores eo iure ea lege uiatores IIII legunto sublegunto, quo iure qua lege q(uaestores), quei nunc sunt, uiatores III legerunt sublegerunt. Quosque quomque quaestores ex lege plebei ue scito praecones legere sublegere oportebit, ei quaestores eo iure ea lege praecones IIII legunto sublegunto, quo iure qua lege quaestores, quei nunc sunt, praecones III legerunt sublegerunt, dum niquem in eis uiatoribus praeconibus legundeis sublegundeis in eius uiatoris praeconis locum uiatorem praeconem legant sublegant, quoius in locum per leges plebeiue scita uiatorem legei sub legi non licebit. Ita que de eis quattuor uiatoribus quaestor queiquomque erit uiatores sumito habeto, utei ante hanc legem rogatam de tribus uiatoribus uiatores habere sumere solitei sunt. . . .

This inscription is nearer Classical than Archaic Latin, and its examples of archaic forms will be understood by reference to the notes on previous inscriptions. With iei cf. *mieis*, No. 46. On siremps see No. 48.

LIV. Epitaphs from the Via Nomentana. (*C.I.L.* I. 1011.)
(*a*) Aurelia L. l. Philematio.

    Uiua Philematium sum Aurelia nominitata,
        Casta, pudens, uolgei nescia, feida uiro.
    uir conleibertus fuit, eidem, quo careo eheu,
        ree fuit ee uero plus superaque parens.
    Septem me naatam annorum gremio ipse recepit,   5
        quadraginta annos nata necis potior.
    ille meo officio adsiduo florebat ad omnis
    *   *   *   *   *   *   *   *   *

(b) L. Aurelius L. l. Hermia lanius de colle Viminale.
haec, quae me faato praecessit, corpore casto,
coniunxs, una meo praedita amans animo,   10
fido fida uiro ueixsit, studio parili qum
nulla in auaritie cessit ab officio.

Notice the doubling of long vowels (cf. *iuus* 'jūs' on the last inscription) v. 4. **supera** 'supra,' a form affected by Lucretius. v. 6. **necis potior**, 'fall into the hands of death.' Cf. the Plautine use of *potior*, e.g. *Capt.* 92 *postquam meus rex est potitus hostium*, 'after my patron fell into the enemy's hands': v. 11 **ueixsit**. The *i* of the first syllable of the Perf. of *vivo* is long by nature, *vīxi;* on *xs* see No. 45, *saxsum;* **qum** is a spelling of *quum* (here possibly the Prep. *cum*), which was common at this time, and which is often found in our Mss. of Plautus, etc. v. 12. **avaritie**. The 5th Decl. form of *avaritia* is used also by Lucretius. Each new generation of poetry brought additions to the 5th Decl. from the ranks of the 1st (see my *Hist. Gram.* ch. iii. § 13).

LV. Inscriptions in honor of Sulla, 82–79 B.C. (*C.I.L.* I. 584–6.)

(a) L. Cornelio L. f. Sullae felIcI dIctatori uIcus laci Fund(ani).
(b) L. Cornelio L. f. Sullae feleici dictatori libertini.
(c) L. Cornelio L. f. Sullae feelio(i) dic.

Notice the tall *i*-form (beside *ei* of **feleici**) to denote the long quantity of the vowel. Long *e* is written *ee* in **feelici**.

LVI. Inscription of the Commune Lyciorum, 81 B.C.? (Greek and Latin.)   (*C.I.L.* I. 589.)

Communi restituto in maiorum leibertatem Roma, Iouei Capitolino et poplo Romano uirtutis beniuolentiae benificique caussa erga Lucios ab communi.

On **poplo** see No. 4. **Caussa** became later *causa*, § 25, *Hist. Gram.* ch. ii. § 9.

LVII. The Furfo Decree, found at Furfo in S. Italy, 58 B.C. (*C.I.L.* I. 603.)

. . . Sei quod ad eam aedem donum datum donatum dedicatumque erit, utei liceat oeti uenum dare. Ubei uenum datum erit, id profanum esto. Venditio locatio aedilis esto, quam quomque ueicus Furfens(is) fecerint, quod se sentiat eam rem sine scelere sine piaculo uendere locare, alis ne potesto. Quae pequnia recepta erit, ea pequnia emere conducere locare dare, quo id templum melius honestiusque seit, liceto. Quae pequnia ad eas res data erit, profana esto, quod d(olo) m(alo) non erit factum. Quod emptum erit aere aut argento ea pequnia, quae pequnia ad id emendum datum erit quod emptum erit, eis rebus eadem lex esto, quasei sei dedicatum sit.

Sei qui heic sacrum surupuerit, aedilis multatio esto, quanti uolet. Idque ueicus Furfens(is) mai(or) pars fifeltares sei apsoluere uolent siue condemnare, liceto.

Sei qui ad hoc templum rem deiuinam fecerit Ioui libero aut Iouis genio, pelleis coria fanei sunto.

alis for *alius*, probably a colloquial form, is found in Catullus (lxvi. 28):—

        quod non fortior ausit alis.

So *alid* in Lucretius i. 263:

        quando alid ex alio reficit natura.

The word **fifeltares** is obscure.

CHAPTER III.

THE AGE OF CICERO AND THE EARLY EMPIRE. CLASSICAL LATIN.

23. The number of Greek words that were being introduced into the language, and the growing study of Greek Grammar and Phonetics, led to the more exact orthography of Greek loan-words. The Greek letters Upsilon (Y, our *y*) and Zeta (Z, our *z*) supplanted the earlier transliteration by *u*, *ss* (*s*) (e.g. *cymba*, earlier *cumba*), and found their way into some words that were pure Latin, e.g. *silva*, wrongly written *sylva*. The Greek Aspirate Mutes were expressed by *th*, *ph*, *ch*, instead of *t*, *p*, *c*, as hitherto, and Greek initial Rho by *rh-*.

24. A change in the 2d Decl. is described by Cicero (*Orat.* xlvi. 155) as having been effected in his own lifetime, viz. the disuse of the old Gen. Plur. ending *-um* (*-om*) for the new-fashioned *-orum* (see my *Hist. Gram.* ch. iii. § 6, and cf. *duonoro(m)*, No. 25).

25. The Orthography of Ciceronian and Augustan Latin exhibits many archaic features that are not always found in our editions of these authors, e.g. *quoi* for *cui*, *ei* frequently for *ī*, *ns* for *s* in *vicensumus*, etc., *u* for *i* in *vicensumus*, *maxumus*, etc. Julius Caesar is said to have brought about the use of the 'new' spelling with *i* on

State inscriptions, *optimus, maximus*. Long Vowels are now indicated by the 'apex,' a mark like the Greek acute accent. Traces of the apex still remain in French, e.g. été, and other alphabets derived from the Latin.

After a diphthong *ll* is now written *l*; while *ss* becomes *s* after a long vowel too, e.g. *causa, misi* (cf. *repromeisserit*, No. 59).

LVIII. Epitaph on an actress, Rome; c. 50 B.C. (*C.I.L.* I. 1009; VI. 10096.)

Eucharis Liciniae l(iberta) docta erodita omnes artes uirgo uixit an(nos) XIIII.

> heus oculo errante quei aspicis léti domus,
> morare gressum et titulum nostrum perlege,
> amor parenteis quem dedit natae suae,
> ubei se reliquiae conlocarent corporis.
> heic uiridis aetas cum floreret artibus
> crescente et aeuo gloriam conscenderet,
> properauit hóra tristis fatalis mea
> et denegauit ultra ueitae spiritum.
> docta, erodita paene Musarum manu,
> quae modo nobilium ludos decoraui choro
> et graeca in scaena prima populo apparui.
> en hoc in tumulo cinerem nostri corporis
> infistae Parcae deposierunt carmine.
> studium patronae, cura, amor, laudes, decus
> silent ambusto corpore et leto tacent.
> reliqui fletum nata genitori meo
> et antecessi, genita post, leti diem.
> bis hic septeni mecum natales dies

tenebris tenentur Ditis aeterna domu.
rogo ut discedens terram mihi dicas leuem.

Early forms on this graceful inscription are **quei, ubei, heic**, and the like. **Deposierunt** shews the older perfect of *pono, posivi* (*posii*), which was in Classical Latin supplanted by *posui;* see on *poseiuei*, No. 44.

Erodita is a pseudo-archaism, for the genuine ancient spelling was, like the classical, with *u*; cf. **exfociont** on the Columna Rostrata, No. 31.

Infistae may with its *i* indicate the close sound of *e* in *infēstus*.

Domus is declined according to the 5th Decl. in l. 1 and l. 19; but in all the early writers we never find it other than a Second Declension Noun; cf. Gk. δόμος.

LIX. Lex Rubria de Civitate Galliae Cisalpinae, on a bronze tablet found in the district of Placentia; 49 B.C. (*C.I.L.* I. 205.)

. . . Qua de re quisque et aquo inGallia cis alpeina damnei infectei exformula restipularei satisue accipere nolet, et ab eo quei ibei i(ure) d(eicundo) p(raerit) postulauerit, idque non k(alumniae) k(aussa) se facere iurauerit; tum is quo d(e) e(a) r(e) inius aditum erit eum quei inius eductus erit d(e) e(a) r(e) exformula repromittere et, sei satis darei debebit, satis dare iubeto decernito. Quei eorum ita non repromeisserit aut non satis dederit, seiquid interim damni datum factum ue ex ea re aut ob e(am) r(em) eoue nomine erit, quam ob rem utei damnei infectei repromissio satisue datio fierei [*iubeatur*] postulatum erit, tum mag(istratus) proue mag(istratu) IIuir

Classical Period. 97

IIIIuir praefec(tus)ue, quoquomque d(e) e(a) r(e) inius aditum erit, d(e) e(a) r(e) ita ius deicito iudicia dato iudicareque iubeto cogito, proinde atque sei d(e) e(a) r(e), quom ita postulatum esset, damnei infectei ex formula recte repromissum satisue datum esset. . . . dum IIuir IIIIuir i(ure) d(eicundo) praefec(tus)ue d(e) e(a) r(e) ius ita deicat curetue, utei ea nomina et municipium colonia locus ineo iudicio, quod ex ieis quae proxsume s(cripta) s(unt) accipietur, includantur concipiantur, quae includei concipei s(ine) d(olo) m(alo) oportere ei uidebuntur, nequid ei quei d(e) e(a) r(e) aget petetue captionei ob e(am) r(em) aut eo nomine esse possit; neiue ea nomina quae inearum qua formula, quae s(upra) s(criptae) s(unt), scripta sunt, aut Mutinam ineo iudicio includei concipei curet, nise iei, quos inter id iudicium accipietur leisue contestabitur, ieis nominibus fuerint, quae in earum qua formula s(cripta) s(unt), et nisei sei Mutinae ea res agetur. Neiue quis mag(istratus) proue mag(istratu) neiue quis pro quo imperio potestateue erit intercedito neiue quid aliud facito, quo minus de ea re ita iudicium detur iudiceturque. . . .

The prevalence of *ei-* forms is in keeping with the archaic character of State inscriptions.

Notice the frequent junction of Prep. and Noun, a practice maintained in Latin Mss. with more or less consistency to the eleventh century or later, **inGallia, inius,** etc.

repromeisserit. On -ss- see § 25.

LX. Lex Julia Municipalis, on three bronze tablets, originally belonging to Heraclea in S. Italy; 45 B.C. (*C.I.L.* I. 206.)

... Quod quemquem h(ac) l(ege) profiterei oportebit, is, apud quem ea professio fiet, eius quei profitebitur nomen et ea quae professus erit et quo die professus sit intabulas publicas referunda curato, eademque omnia quae uteique intabulas rettulerit ita intabulam in album referunda curato, idque aput forum et, quom frumentum populo dabitur, ibei ubei frumentum populo debitur cottidie maiorem partem diei propositum habeto, u(nde) d(e) p(lano) r(ecte) l(egi) p(ossit).

Queiquomque frumentum populo dabit damdumue curabit, nei quoi eorum, quorum nomina h(ac) l(ege) ad co(n)s(ulem) pr(aetorem) tr(ibunum) pl(ebis) intabula inalbo proposita erunt, frumentum dato neue dare iubeto neue sinito. Quei ad uersus ea eorum quoi frumentum dederit, is in tr(itici) m(odios) I HS IƆƆƆ populo dare damnas esto eiusque pecuniae quei uolet petitio esto.

... Quemquomque ante suum aedificium uiam publicam h(ac) l(ege) tueri oportebit, quei eorum eam uiam arbitratu eius aed(ilis), quoius oportuerit, non tuebitur, eam uiam aed(ilis), quoius arbitratu eam tuerei oportuerit, tuemdam locato. Isque aed(ilis) diebus ne minus X antequam locet aput forum ante tribunale suom propositum habeto, quam uiam tuendam et quo die locaturus sit et quorum ante aedificium ea uia sit. Eisque, quorum ante aedificium ea uia erit, procuratoribusue eorum domum denuntietur facito se eam uiam locaturum et quodie locaturus sit. Eamque locationem palam in foro per q(uaestorem) urb(anum) eumue quei aerario praerit facito. Quamta pecunia eam uiam locauerit, tamtae pecuniae eum eosque, quorum ante aedificium ea uia erit proportioni, quamtum quoiusque ante aedificium uiae inlongitudine et inlatitudine erit, q(uaestor) urb(anus) queiue aerario praerit intabulas publicas pecuniae factae referendum curato. Ei, quei eam uiam tuemdam redemerit, tamtae pecuniae eum eosue ad tribuito sine d(olo) m(alo). Sei is quei ad tributus erit eam pecuniam diebus XXX proxumeis, quibus ipse aut procurator eius sciet adtributionem factam esse, ei, quoi ad tributus erit, non soluerit neque satis fecerit, is quamtae pecuniae ad tributus erit, tamtam pecuniam et eius dimidium ei, quoi ad tributus erit, dare debeto. Inque eam rem is quo quomque de ea re aditum erit iudicem iudiciumue ita dato utei depecunia credita iudicem iudiciumue dari oporteret.

. . . Quae plostra noctu in urbem inducta erunt, quominus ea plostra inania aut stercoris ex portandei caussa post solem ortum h(oris) X diei bubus iumenteis ue iuncta in u(rbe) R(oma) et ab u(rbe) R(oma) p(assus) M esse liceat, e(ius) h(ac) l(ege) n(ihil) r(ogatur).

. . . Quae loca serueis publiceis ab cens(oribus) habitandei utendei caussa ad tributa sunt, ei quominus eis loceis utantur, e(ius) h(ac) l(ege) n(ihil) r(ogatur).

Queiquomque inmunicipieis coloneis praefectureis foreis conciliabuleis c(iuium) R(omanorum) IIuir(ei) IIIIuir(ei) erunt alioue quo nomine mag(istratum) potestatemue sufragio eorum, quei quoiusque municipi coloniae praefecturae fori conciliabuli erunt, habebunt, neiquis eorum quem in eo municipio colonia praefectura foro conciliabulo in senatum decuriones conscriptosue legito neue sublegito neue coptato neue recitandos curato nisi indemortuei damnateiue locum eiusue quei confessus erit se senatorem decurionem conscreiptumue ibei h(ac) l(ege) esse non licere.

. . . Qui pluribus inmunicipieis coloneis praefectureis domicilium habebit et is Romae census erit, quo magis in municipio colonia praefectura h(ac) l(ege) censeatur, e(ius) h(ac) l(ege) n(ihil) r(ogatur).

Quei lege pl(ebei) ue sc(ito) permissus est fuit, utei leges in municipio fundano municipibusue eius municipi daret, sei quid is post h(anc) l(egem) r(ogatam) ineo anno proxumo, quo h(anc) l(egem) populus iuserit, adeas leges addiderit commutauerit conrexerit, municipis fundanos item teneto, utei oporterit, sei eas res abeo tum, quom primum leges eis municipibus lege pl(ebei) ue sc(ito) dedit, adeas leges additae commutatae conrectae essent. Neue quis intercedito neue quid facito, quo minus ea rata sint quoue minus municipis fundanos teneant eisque optemperetur.

Julius Caesar, like Augustus and some succeeding Emperors, found time for the study of Grammar amidst the cares of government. We may be sure that the orthography of any of his laws would be carefully revised by him; so that we have here the way in which a Grammarian, who was at the same time a man of the world, judged that Latin words should be written in a formal document. That Caesar did not scruple to introduce the forms of spoken Latin into State inscriptions we know from the fact that it was he who effected the adoption of spellings like *optimus, maximus* (with *i* for the older *u*) in inscriptions of the kind. (Quint. I. vii. 21 'optimus maximus,' ut mediam i litteram, quae veteribus u fuerat, acciperent, Gai primum Caesaris inscriptione traditur factum.)

The Prep. and Noun (Adj.) often form a word-group, as in *denuo* (*de novo*), etc., e.g. **intabulas.**

damnās is a form of *damnatus* affected in legal phraseology. It seems to represent an I-stem *damnati-*, like *Sanates* (a legal term for allies who had revolted but afterwards returned to their allegiance, 'quasi sana mente') beside *sanati*, *Manes* beside O. Lat. *mano-* and the like. *Damnatis became *damnas*, as the Plautine forms *nostratis*, *Arpinatis*, etc., became *nostras*, *Arpinas*. A curious spelling (due to an etymological theory?) is the use of *m* for *n* in the Gerund and Gerundive, e.g. **tuemdam**, also in **tamtam**, etc. Notice also **aput**, on which see § 20.

LXI. Glandes, found at Perusia; 41–40 B.C. (*C.I.L.* I. 685, 692.)

(*a*) L. Antoni Calui peristi O. Caesarus uictoria.

(*b*) Esureis et me celas.

These sentences were carved by soldiers on the leaden bullets which they shot against the defenders of Perusia, in the course of the long blockade of L. Antonius by Octavianus. They shew us how Latin was written by uneducated Romans at that period. Notice the spelling **esureis** with *ei* for later *ī*, and the retention in plebeian Latin of the old Gen. ending *-ŏs* (*-ŭs*) of the 3d Decl., **Caesarus** (§ 10). The first sentence has an echo of a Trochaic Septenarius. This was the popular metre at this time, and in uneducated hands was generally constructed with regard to accent rather than to quantity.

Two interesting monuments of Augustus follow, the official proclamation about the Ludi Saeculares, and the autobiographical notice of the Emperor. They should be compared with the Law of Julius Caesar (No. 60), and the Decree of the Emperor Claudius (No. 64).

LXII. Commentarius Ludorum Saecularium, found recently in the bed of the Tiber. (*Ephemeris Epigraphica*, VIII. ii.)

. . . Ludique noctu sacrificio confecto sunt commissi in scaena quoi theatrum adiectum non fuit nullis positis sedilibus, centumque et X matronae quibus denuntiatum erat XVuirorum uerbis sellisternia habuerunt Iunoni et Dianae duabus sellis positis.

K. Iun. in Capitolio bouem marem Ioui optimo maximo proprium inmolauit imp. Caesar Augustus, ibidem alterum M. Agrippa, precati autem sunt ita:

Iuppiter optime maxime uti tibi in illeis libreis scriptum est quarumque rerum ergo quodque melius siet populo R. Quiritibus tibi hoc boue mare pulchro sacrum fiat te quaeso precorque; cetera uti supra.

Ad atallam fuerunt Caesar Agrippa Scaeuola Sentius Lollius Asinius Gallus Rebilus.

Deinde ludi Latini in theatro ligneo quod erat constitutum in campo secundum Tiberim sunt commissi, eodemque modo sellisternia matres familiae habuerunt, neque sunt ludi intermissi iei qui noctu coepti erant fieri et edictum propositum.

XV uir s. f. dic.:

Cum bono more et proinde celebrato frequentibus exsemplis, quandocumque iusta laetitiae publicae caussa fuit, minui luctus matronarum placuerit, idque tam sollemnium sacrorum ludorumque tempore referri diligenterque opseruari pertinere uideatur et ad honorem deorum et ad memoriam cultus eorum: statuimus offici nostri esse per edictum denuntiare feminis, uti luctum minuant.

Noctu autem ad Tiberim sacrificium fecit deis Ilithyis libeis VIIII popanis VIIII pthoibus VIIII imp. Caesar Augustus; precatus est hoc modo:

Ilithyia, utei tibei in illeis libreis scriptum est, quarumque rerum ergo, quodque melius siet p. R. Quiritibus, tibi VIIII popanis et VIIII libeis et VIIII pthoibus sacrum fiat; te quaeso precorque.

IV nonas Iun. in Capitolio inmolauit Iunoni reginae bouem feminam imp. Caesar Augustus, ibidem alteram M. Agrippa et precatus est hoc modo:

Iuno regina, uti tibi in illis libris scriptum est, quarumque rerum ergo quodque melius siet p. R. Quiritibus, tibi boue femina pulchra sacrum fiat; te quaeso precorque.

Deinde CX matribus familias nuptis, quibus denu[ntiatum fuit ut conuenirent, imp. Caesar Augustus] praeit in haec uerba:

Iuno regina, ast quid est quod melius siet p. R. Quiritibus . . . Sacrificioque perfecto pueri XXVII quibus denuntiatum erat patrimi et matrimi et puellae totidem carmen cecinerunt; eodemque modo in Capitolio . . .

Carmen composuit Q. Horatius Flaccus. . . .

In connection with this interesting record of Augustus' reign, the *Carmen Saeculare* of Horace should be read. **atallam** is obscure. The word has been connected with *attānus (atanus?)*, a vessel used for sacrificial purposes. It may be a Diminutive; cf. *Hispallus* from *Hispānus*.

Notice the spellings **quoi** (the form in use even in

104 *Handbook of Latin Inscriptions.*

Quintilian's time), **illeis libeis** and the frequent use of *ei*, **exsemplis, opseruari** the phonetic spelling, while *obs-* was the grammatical, **pthoibus**. The last example exhibits the normal mode of expressing a Greek aspirate group in classical Latin. We should write *pthisis*, not *phthisis*, *dipthongus*, not *diphthongus*, etc.

LXIII. The Monumentum Ancyranum or Res Gestae Divi Augusti, from the wall of a temple at Ancyra (edited by Mommsen).

Rérum gestárum díuí Augusti, quibus orbem terrarum imperio populi Rom(ani) subiécit, et inpensarum, quas in rem publicam populumque Romanum fecit, incísarum in duabus aheneís pílís, quae sunt Romae positae, exemplar subiectum. Rés publica ne quid detrimenti caperet, me pro praetore simul cum consulibus prouidere iussit. Populus autem eódem anno mé consulem, cum co(n)s(ul) uterque bello occidisset, et trium uirum reí publicae constituendae creauit.

Quí parentem meum interfecerunt, eós in exilium expulí iudiciís legitimís ultus eórum facinus, et posteá bellum inferentís reí publicae uící bis acie.

Bella terra et mari ciuilia externaque tóto in orbe terrarum suscepi uictorque omnibus superstitibus cíuibus pepercí. Externas gentés, quibus túto ignosci potuit, conseruáre quam excídere malui. Míllia ciuium Rómanorum adacta sacrámento meo fuerunt circiter quingenta. Ex quibus dedúxi in coloniás aut remísi in municipia sua stipendis emeritis millia aliquantum plura quam trecenta et iís omnibus agrós a me emptos aut pecuniam pró praediis a me dedí. Naues oépi sescentas praeter eás, si quae minóres quam triremes fuerunt.

Classical Period.

Bis ouáns triumphaui, tris egi curulís triumphós, et appellátus sum uiciens semel imperátor. Cum deinde plúris triumphos mihi senatus decreuisset, eis supersedi. Item saepe laurus deposuí, in Capitolio uotis, quae quóque bello nuncupaueram, solutís. Ob res á me aut per legatos meós auspicís meis terra marique prospere gestás quinquagiens et quinquiens decreuit senátus supplicandum esse dís immortalibus. Dies autem, per quós ex senátús consulto supplicátum est, fuere DCCCLXXXX. In triumphis meis ducti sunt ante currum meum regés aut regum liberi nouem. Consul fueram terdeciens, cum scribebam haec, at agebam septimum et trigensimum annum tribuniciae potestatis.

Dictaturam et apsenti et praesenti mihi datam . . . a populo et senatu M. Marcello et L. Arruntio consulibus non accepi. Non recusaui in summa frumenti penuria curationem annonae, quam ita administraui, ut . . . paucis diebus metu et periclo quo erat populum uniuersum meis impensis liberarem. Consulatum tum datum annuum et perpetuum non accepi.

. . . .

Patriciórum numerum auxí consul quintum iussú populi et senátús. Senatum ter légi. In consulátú sexto cénsum populi conlegá M. Agrippá égí. Lústrum post annum alterum et quadragensimum féci. Quó lústro ciuium Románórum censa sunt capita quadragiens centum millia et sexaginta tria millia. Iterum consulari cum imperio lústrum sólus féci C. Censorino et C. Asinio cos. Quó lústro censa sunt ciuium Romanórum capita quadragiens centum millia et ducenta triginta tria millia. Tertium consulári cum imperio lústrum conlegá Tib. Caesare filio feci Sex. Pompeio et Sex. Appuleio cos. Quó lústro censa sunt ciuium Románórum capitum quadragiens centum millia et nongenta triginta et septem millia. Legibus nouis latis com-plura exempla maiorum exolescentia iam ex nostro usu reduxi et ipse multárum rérum exempla imitanda posteris traditi.

Vota pro ualetudine mea suscipi per consulés et sacerdotes quinto quoque anno senatus decreuit. Ex iis uotís saepe fecerunt uíuo me ludos aliquotiens sacerdotum quattuor amplissima collégia aliquotiens consules. Priuatim etiam et múnicipatim úniuersi ciues sacrificauerunt semper apud omnia puluínária pró ualetudine mea.

Nomen meum senatus consulto inclusum est in saliáre carmen, et sacrosanctus ut essem . . . et ut quoad uíuerem, tribúnicia potestás mihí esset, lege sanctum est. Pontifex maximus ne fierem in uíuí conlegae locum, populo id sacerdotium deferente mihi, quod pater meus habuit, recusaui. Cepi id sacerdotium aliquod post annós eó mortuo qui ciuilis motus occasione occupauerat, cuncta ex Italia ad Comitia mea . . . tanta multitudine, quanta Romae nunquam antea fuisse fertur, coeunte P. Sulpicio C. Valgio consulibus.

Aram Fortunae reduci iuxta aedés Honoris et Virtutis ad portam Capenam pro reditu meo senátus consacrauit, in qua pontifices et uirgines Vestales anniuersárium sacrificium facere iussi die, quo consulibus Q. Lucretio et M. Vinucio in urbem ex Syria redi, et diem Augustalia ex cognomine nostro appellauit. . . .

The spelling of an inscription of this sort would, we may be sure, be carefully looked after; for Augustus was noted for his attention to orthography and other points of grammar. The apex of **dedúxi** shews us that the *u* of the Perf. of *duco* was pronounced long like the *u* of the Pres. (cf. **lústrum**). Notice **apsenti** (cf. **opseruari** of the Comm. Lud. Saec.).

LXIV. Inscription of the Emp. Claudius at Lyons.

... Equidem prímam omnium illam cogitationem hominum quam maxime prímam occursuram mihi prouideo. Deprecor, ne quasi nouam istam rem introduci exhorrescatis, sed illa potius cogitetis quam multa in háo cíuitate nouata sint et quidem statim ab origine urbis nostrae in quod formas statúsque rés p(ublica) nostra díducta sit.

Quondam réges hanc tenuére urbem, nec tamen domesticis successoribus eam tradere contigit. Superuenere alieni et quidam externí ut Numa Romulo successerit ex Sabinís ueniéns, uícinus quidem, sed tunc externus; ut Ancó Márcio Príscus Tarquinius, propter temeratum sanguinem,—quod patre Demaratho Corinthio natus erat et Tarquiniensi mátre generosá sed inopí ut quae tali marito necesse habuerit succumbere,—cum domi repelleretur á gerendís honoribus, postquam Romam migrauit regnum adeptus est. Huic quoque et filio nepotiue eius, nam et hoc inter auctores discrepat, insertus Seruius Tullius, si nostros sequimur captiua natus Ocresiá, sí Tuscos Caeli quondam Vinennae sodalis fidelissimus omnisque eius cásús comes; postquam uariá fortuna exáctus cum omnibus reliquís Caeliáni exercitús Etrúriá excessit montem Caelium occupauit et aduce suó Caelio ita appellitatus mutatóque nomine, nam Tusce Mastarna eí nomen erat, ita appellatus est ut díxi, et regnum summá cum reí p(ublicae) útilitate optinuit. Deinde, postquam Tarquini Superbí móres inuísi cíuitati nostrae esse coeperunt qua ipsius qua filiorum eius, nempe pertaesum est mentés régni et ad consules annuós magistrátús administratio reí p(ublicae) tránslata est.

Quid nunc commemorem dictaturae hóc ipso consulári imperium ualentius repertum apud maiores nostros quo in asperioribus bellís aut in cíuili motú difficiliore uterentur, aut in auxilium plebis creatós tribunos plébei ? Quid áconsulibus ad decemuiros translátum imperium, solutoque postea decemuirali régno ad consules rúsus reditum ? Quid in plurís distributum consulare imperium tribunosque militum consulari imperio appellatós. qui séni et saepe octoni crearentur ? Quid communicátos postrémo cum plebe honóres non imperi solum sed sacerdotiorum quoque ? Iam si nárrem bella á quibus coeperint maiores nostri et quo processerimus, uereor né nimió insolentior esse uidear et quaesisse iactatiónem glóriae prolati imperi ultrá óceanum, sed illoc potius reuertar cíuitatem . . . potest sane nouo more et díuus Augustus auonculus meus et patruus Ti. Caesar omnem flórem ubique coloniárum ac municipiorum bonórum scilicet uirorum et locupletium in háo cúria esse uoluit. Quid ergo! non Italicus senator prouinciali potior est ? Iam uobís cum hanc partem censurae meae adprobáre coepero quid de eáré sentiam rebus ostendam, sed ne prouinciales quidem simodo ornare curiam poterint reiciendos puto.

Ornátissima ecce colonia ualentissimaque Viennensium quam longo iam tempore senatores huic curiae confert, ex qua colonia inter paucos equestris órdinis órnamentum L. Vestínum familiarissime díligo et hodieque in rebus meís detineo, cuius líberí fruantur, quaesó, primo sacerdotiorum gradú, post modo cum annís promoturi dignitatis suae incrementa. Ut dírum nomen latronis taceam, et odi illud palaestricum pródigium quod ante in domum consulatum intulit quam colonia sua solidum cíuitatis Romanae benificium cónsecuta est. Idem dé frátre eius possum dícere miserabili quidem indignissimoque hóc cású ut uobís utilis senator esse non possit.

Tempus est iam, Ti. Caesar Germanice, detegere té patribus conscriptís quo tendat oratio tua ; iam enim ad extremos fínes Galliae Narbonensis uenistí.

Tot ecce insignes iuuenes quot intueor non magis sunt paenitendi senatores quam paenitet Persicum nobilissimum uirum amicum meum inter imagines maiorum suorum Allobrogici nomen legere. Quod si haec ita esse consentitis quid ultrá desideratis quam ut uobís digito demonstrem solum ipsum ultra fínes prouinciae Narbonensis iam uobís senatores mittere quando ex Luguduno habere nos nostri ordinis uiros non paenitet. Timide quidem, p(atres) c(onscripti), egressus adsuetos familiares que uobís prouinciarum terminos sum, sed destricte iam comatae Galliae causa agenda est, inqua siquis hoc intuetur quod bello per decem annos exercuerunt díuom Iulium, ídem opponat centum annorum immóbilem fidem obsequiumque multís trepidís rebus nostrís, plusquam expertum illi patri meo Druso Germaniam subigenti tutam quiete sua secúramque átergo pácem praestiterunt, et quidem cum adcensus nouo tum opere et in ad sueto Gallís ad bellum auocatus esset, quod opus quam arduum sit nobís nunc cum maxime, quam uís nihil ultra quam ut publice notae sint facultates nostrae exquiratur, nimis magno experimento cognoscimus.

Claudius, too, made a hobby of grammatical studies, so that this inscription is valuable evidence for the orthography of the period. The account of Servius Tullius is an interesting contribution to early Roman history. Notice nárrem, díxi, which shew that the first syllable in each of these words had a long vowel. (Cf. on *naro*, No. 73.)

The eruption of Vesuvius in 79 A.D. destroyed Herculaneum and Pompeii. In the ruins of Herculaneum a collection of papyrus rolls, the books of the period, was found, some of them in Latin. At Pompeii, besides actual inscriptions, many 'graffiti,' i.e. sentences scratched on a wall by idlers, have come to light. They shew the careless illiterate spelling of the day, as the papyri the literary orthography.

LXV. Herculanean Papyrus, containing the 'Incerti de Augusti Bello Aegyptiaco Carmen' (ed. Baehrens, *Poet. Lat. Min.* vol. i., p. 218).

... Praeberetque suae spectacula tristia mortis.
    Qualis adínstantís aciés cum tela parantur,
    Signa, tubae, classesque simul terrestribus armís,
    Est facies ea uisa locí cum saeua coirent
    Ínstrumenta necis uario congesta paratú.
    Undique sic illúc campo deforme coactum
    Omne uagabatur leti genus, omne timoris
... Aut pendente suis ceruícibus aspide, mollem
    Labitur in somnum trahiturque libídine mortis.
    Perculit afflatu breuis hunc sine morsibus anguis
    Volnere seu tenui; pars inlita parua uenéni
    Ocius interemit, laqueís pars cogitur artís
    Intersaeptam animam pressís effundere uenis.
    Immersisque freto clauserunt guttura fauces.
                   ... nec urbem
Opsidione tamen nec corpora moenibus arcent,
Castraque promuris atque arma pedestria ponunt.
    Hos intercoetus talisque ad bella paratús
Utraque sollemnis iterum reuocauerat orbes.
Cónsiliís nox apta ducum, lux aptior armis.

LXVI. Pompeian Graffiti.

(1) Accompanying a picture of gladiators. (*C.I.L.* IV. 538.)

Tetraites Prudes . . . Abiat Venere Bompeiiana iratam qui hoc laesaerit.

Tetraites, Prudens . . . Habeat Venerem Pompeianam iratam qui hoc laeserit.

The famous gladiator Tetraites, or in the Oscan form Petraites, is known from Petronius, c. 52: nam Hermerotis pugnas et Petraitis in poculis habeo, and c. 71: valde te rogo, ut secundum pedes statuae meae catellam fingas et coronas et unguenta et Petraitis omnes pugnas.

Misspellings like *abiat*, with mute *h* and confusion of *e* and *i*, *laesaerit*, with confusion of *ae* and *e*, reflect the pronunciation of the populace (partly Greek, partly Oscan, partly foreign and servile) of Pompeii. In time these depraved forms found their way into the speech of the capital, and at last even into literary Latin (§ 26).

(2) (*C.I.L.* IV. 650.)

Gauium Rufum IIuir(um) o(ro) f(aciatis).

Gāvio- is the Oscan form of the name *Gāio-*.

(3) (*C.I.L.* IV. 882.)

Pilocalus uotum sol(uit) libes merito.

On **libes** for *libens* see § 22.

(4) Trochaic Septenarius, on wall of room in house of Sallust. (*C.I.L.* IV. 1234.)

Bupa que bela is tibi me misit qui tuus est uale.
pupa, quae bella es, tibi me misit qui tuus est: uale.
On **que** for *quae*, cf. *laesaerit* above (1).

(5) Lines from Ovid, *A.A.* i. 475 sq., on the wall of a law-court. (*C.I.L.* IV. 1895.)

quid pote tan durum saxso aut quid mollius unda?
dura tamen molli saxsa cauantur aqua.

Ovid's lines begin: *quid magis est saxo durum aut,* etc. On *xs* for *x* see on *saxsum*, No. 45.

Tan for *tam* may reflect the vague sound of final *-m*, which shewed its presence only in the nasal tone it gave to the preceding vowel (§ 20), or it may be due to the pronunciation in one word-group of the Adv. and Adj. *tam-durum.* Cf. *etiannunc* for *etiam nunc*, a spelling mentioned by Roman Grammarians and found on a Herculanean papyrus.

(6) Lines on the wall of a law-court. (*C.I.L.* IV. 1824.)

quisquis amat, ueniat. Veneri uolo frangere costas
 fustibus et lumbos debilitare deae.
si potest illa mihi tenerum pertundere pectus,
quit ego non possim caput illae frangere fuste?

v. 3. *potĕst*, though not allowed by the classical poets, no doubt represented the everyday pronunciation at this time, as it did in the time of Plautus and the early Dramatists, who freely admit this scansion.

v. 4. *quit* (= *quid*, § 20), to be metrical, should be *cur; illae* was a current by-form of *illi*, Dat. Sg. Fem.

(7) Lines on the wall of a law-court. (*C.I.L.* IV. 2487.)

admiror, paries, te non cecidisse ruina,
qui tot scriptorum taedia sustineas.

This is a specimen of the correct Latin of the time, differing in no respect from the orthography of our text-books.

CHAPTER IV.

IMPERIAL AND LATE LATIN.

26. To this period belongs the gradual decay of Latin, and its passage into the Romance languages of modern Europe. It is, unfortunately, hardly possible to get from inscriptions a clear and connected account of the downward progress of the language. For it was from the spoken language of the Roman Provinces that the Romance languages arose; while it is the written or literary language that is presented to us, more or less correctly according to the education of the maker of the inscription, or the locality to which it belongs, in inscriptions and in documents. It is the deviations from standard Latin on these inscriptions which give us a glimpse at the actual spoken Latin of the place and time; but this spoken language, Vulgar-Latin as it is usually called, never wholly reveals itself to us until it appears as a fully developed Romance language—Italian, French, Spanish, and the like. A Latin word like **bĭbĭt** is, in Italian, beve, the Latin ĭ having been replaced by e (close e, the vowel of French été), and the Latin intervocalic b by v, while the t, at first retained before a vowel initial (cf. Fr. 'il vien(t),' but 'vient-il?'; 'il a' but 'a-t-il?'), has finally been dropped in all circumstances. The pronunciation beve(t) (with v sounded like our w) was probably a very old one, but the only trace of it that we could expect to find on an inscription would be that the word would now and then be written bebit, or bibet or bive, or bevi, or even (the phonetically correct spelling) beve, though in the great majority of instances it would be written in accordance with the rules of the grammatical handbooks of the time, *bibit*. It is, then, to the faulty spellings of late Latin inscriptions that we must look for information about the actual spoken language of the period.

27. Here are the chief faults that we find: —

(1) *e* and *ae* (also *oe*) are confused.

(2) *e* and *i*, *o* and *u*, are confused.

(3) final consonants are dropped; *m*, e.g. *vino* (Ital. vino) for *vinum*, *pace* (Ital. pace) for *pacem* ; *s*, e.g. *advocato* (Ital. advocato) for *advocatus* ; *t*, e.g. Ital. beve (see above).

(4) hand in hand with this loss of the case-endings went the confusion of cases and the expression of all cases by one case-form.

To distinguish the Gen. and Dat. a Prep. was used, e.g. *de vino* Gen., *a(d) vino* Dat. (Fr. de vin and à vin).

(5) *b* and *v* are confused.

(6) *h* is wrongly omitted or inserted.

(7) *x* and *s* are confused.

(8) *ct* and *tt* (*t*) are confused.

(9) *c* and *q* are confused.

(10) In the Verb, Auxiliaries like *habeo, vado*, take the place of Tense suffixes.

(11) *f* for Gk. φ. By the fifth century A.D. Gk. φ had become a spirant, as it is in mod. Gk.

(12) *ci* and *ti* are confused when a vowel follows.
(13) *sc* and *ss* are confused before *e, i*.
(14) *i(e)* was prefixed to initial *st, sp, sc*.

28. The change in the pronunciation of *c* before the *e* and *i* vowels is an important change. In speaking of it we must carefully distinguish between *c* in a word like *centum, civitas*, and *c* in a word like *uncia*. It was in the latter class of words where *ci (ce)* was followed by a vowel that the assibilation of *c* first began. *Ti (te)* in a similar situation was assibilated in the same way, so that *nuntius, uncia*, etc., came to be pronounced as a disyllable with some *s*-sound at the beginning of the second syllable. The Romance words from Latin *platĕa*, a (wide) street, may be cited as examples of the change, Ital. piazza, Span. plaza, Fr. place. This palatalization of *ti* and *ci* in hiatus (i.e. before another vowel) may be referred to the fourth and fifth centuries A.D. The assibilation of *c* (not *t*) before *e, i*, when these vowels were followed by a consonant, came much later, about the sixth and seventh centuries (cf. Ital. cento, città, with *c* sounded like our *ch* of 'church,' Fr. cent, cité). *G* assumed before *e, i* the sound of *y* at a somewhat earlier period; and before other vowels *g* became, when pretonic, a mere spirant like *g* of German 'Tage,' and so is often omitted in writing, e.g. *frualitas* for *frugalitas, A(u)(g)ustus*, whence Fr. Août. (See my *Hist. Gram.* ch. ii. § 7.)

29. Another change that passed over the language was the gradual loss of the distinction of quantity under the influence of the stress accentuation. An accentuated vowel, we may roughly say, became long, an unaccented, short; e.g. *ŏrātor, pīper* for *ōrātor, pĭper*. Or rather the different vowels of a word came to have more or less the same length (much as is the case in modern Italian), and the distinction between vowels was rather qualitative than quantitative. $\bar{E}$ was 'close' *e* (rather than 'long' *e*) and was merged in the neighbouring sound $\bar{\imath}$. $\breve{E}$ was 'open' *e* (rather than 'short' *e*) and was merged in *ae*. So with $\breve{u}$ and $\bar{o}$. Quantitative Metre thus became an artificial branch of poetry, no longer reflecting the actual educated pronunciation, and Accentual Metre takes its place more or less completely according to the education of the writer.

30. Syncope, too, attacked every short post-tonic or pre-tonic syllable and changed the whole aspect of the language. Lat. *vetŭlus* became *vetlus, veclus* (Ital. vecchio), *sīmia* became *simya* (Fr. singe), *ăpium* became *apyum* (Fr. ache), *cambiare* became *cambyare* (Fr. changer). (*Hist. Gram.* ch. ii. § 7.) This fact must be borne in mind in reading the rude accentual or half-accentual metres of later Latin; e.g. pronounce *potyones* (No. 69).

LXVII. Wax-Tablet relating to the abolition of a 'collegium funeraticium,' Dacia, 167 A.D. (*C.I.L.* III. ii. p. 927.)

. . . Iulium Iuli quoque commagistrum suum ex die magisteri sui non accessisse ad Alburnum neque in collegio: seque eis qui presentes fuerunt rationem reddedisse et si quit eorum abuerat reddedisset siue funeribus et cautionem suam in qua eis cauerat, recepisset: modoque autem neque funeraticis sufficerent neque loculum aberet neque quisquam tam magno tempore diebus

118   *Handbook of Latin Inscriptions.*

quibus legi continetur conuenire uoluerint aut conferre funera-
ticia siue munera: seque idcirco per hunc libellum publice
testantur, ut, si quis defunctus fuerit, ne putet se collegium
abere aut ab eis aliquem petitionem funeris abiturum. . . .

Late spellings are **presentes, reddedisse,** etc., **abuerat,**
etc. On **quit** for *quid*, see § 20.

LXVIII. Epitaph in rude Hexameters on a Pannonian
soldier. Found at Rome. End of second century A.D.
(*Eph. Epigr.* IV. 346, 936.)

    respice praeteriens, uiator, consobrini pietate parata;
    cum lacrimis statui, quanto in munere posto uidetis.
    Pannonia terra creat, tumulat Italia tellus.
    annis XXVI, ut sibi castris honorem atquireret ipse,
    dolori magno substentauit tempore longo.
    postea cum sperans dolorem effugisse nefandam,
    ante diem meritum hunc demersit at Styga Pluton.
    quotsi fata eo sinuissent luce uidere,
    ista prius triste munus posui dolore repletus,
    munus inane quidem. terra nunc diuidit ista
    ossua sub titulo potius. tu opta, uiator,
    cum pietate tua ipso terra leue, nobis fortuna beata,
    ex qua tu possis obitus bene linquere nato

Val. Antonius et Aur. Victorinus hered(es) Ulpio Quintiano
eq(uiti) sing(ulari) ben(e) mer(ito) posuer(unt).

l. 2. *quantum in munere positum.* l. 4. A service of
25 years would entitle him to a 'missio honesta.' l. 6.
cum sperans, 'when hoping.' l. 8. *eum siuissent lucem
uidere.* l. 12. *ipsi terram leuem, nobis fortunam beatam.*
l. 13. *natum.*

LXIX. Epitaph in rude Hexameters from Carthage. End of second century A.D. or later. (*C.I.L.* VIII. 1027.)

Vitalis Aug. n(ostri) tabellarius, uiuet et conuiuat. Et Antigona, uiuet et conuiuatur.
 dum sum Vitalis et uiuo, ego feci sepulcrhum
 adque meos uersus, dum transseo, perlego et ipse.
 diploma circaui totam regione pedestrem
 et canibus prendi lepores et denique uulpes.
 postea potiones calicis perduxi libenter,
 multa iuuentutis feci, quia sum moriturus.
 quisque sapis iuuenis, uiuo tibi pone sepulcrhum.

This thoroughly pagan epitaph of a lusty postman, who bore the not inappropriate name of Vitalis, has some points of linguistic interest. Notice (1) the doubt about the spelling of the *chr* of *sepulchrum*, (2) *adque* for *atque*, (3) the pronunciation of Gk. δίπλωμα as *diplŏma*, the stress accent on the first syllable having shortened the second as in Mod. Greek, and its declension in everyday speech as a Latin A-stem (cf. *schema, -ae*, Plaut.), (4) trisyllabic *potyones* (§ 30), etc., etc. In v. 7. *quisque* has its O. Lat. sense of *quicunque;* v. 3, *circare* (for *circuire*) is the prototype of Fr. chercher; *regione(m) pedestrem* is the district assigned to the foot postal service as opposed to the mail-coach service.

LXX. Acrostic epitaph in rude Hexameters, from Tunis. Second or third century A.D. (*C.I.L.* VIII. 152.)

 Urbanilla mihi coniunx uerecundia plena hic sita est
 Romae comes negotiorum socia parsimonio fulta.

bene gestis omnibus cum in patria mecum rediret,
au miseram Carthago mihi eripuit sociam.
nulla spes uiuendi mihi sine coniuge tali:
illa domum seruare meam, illa et consilio iuuare.
luce priuata misera quescit in marmore clusa.
Lucius ego coniunx hic te marmore texi
Anc nobis sorte dedit fatu, cum luci daremur.

l. 4. **au**, Interj.   l. 9. *hanc nobis sortem dedit fatum.*

LXXI. Epitaph in Hexameters from Nicopolis on the Danube. Third century. (*C.I.L.* III. 754; suppl. 7436.)

floribus ut saltem requiescant membra iucundis
Aeliae carae mihi nunc hoc inclusae sepulcro,
regina Ditis magni regis, precor hoc te —
nam meruit haec multa suis pro laudibus a me —
inmeritae propere soluentem fila dearum,
quae globo Parcarum reuoluta cuncta gubernant.
qualis enim fuerit uita, quam deinde pudica,
si possem effari, cithara suadere ego Manes.
haec primum casta, quot te audire libenter
et mundi spatia, Ditis quoque regia, norunt.
hanc precor Elysiis iubeas consistere campis
et myrta redimire comas et tempora flore.
Lar mihi haec quondam, haec spes, haec unica uita,
et uellet quod uellem, nollet quoque ac si ego nollem,
intima nulla ei quae non mihi nota fuere,
nec labos huic defuit, nec uellerum inscia fila,
parca manu set larga meo in amore mariti,
nec sine me cibus huic gratus nec munera Bacchi,

consilio mira, cata mente, nobili fama.
carmini, possessor, faueas precor, ac precor ut tu
hanc tituli sedem uelles decorare quodannis
et foueas aeui monumentum tempore grato,
roscida si rosula seu grato flore amaranthi
et multis generum pomis uariisque nouisque,
ut possit toto refoueri temporis anno.

l. 5. **inmeritae**, sc. Aeliae, **soluentem**, sc. reginam Ditis.
l. 8. **suadere** = *suaderem*. l. 9. **quot** = *quod*, cf. l. 17. **set**.
l. 21. **quodannis**. (§ 20.) l. 24. for **multum generum** or **multig**.

LXXII. Epitaph in Hexameters, from Rome. 348 A.D. (Rossi, *Inscr. Christ. Rom.* I. 64, 101.)

felix uita uiri, felicior exitus ipse.
Caiani semper crescit per saecula nomen,
nescit fama mori sed semper uibit ubique.
aduenit hospes princeps Romanus in urbem,
qui fuit hic primum iuris consultor amicus.

Quiescit in pacem depositus diem quartum nonas Augustas Flauio Filippo et Flauio Sallea consulibus: pater Sabbatius fecit.

l. 3. **uibit** = *vivit* (§ 27). l. 4. In late poetry an initial *h* makes a preceding short syllable long by position. This was an arbitrary usage of poets in imitation of Virgil's *terga fatigamus hasta*, where, however, -*mūs* is really a case of lengthening in arsi. Initial *h* was scarcely sounded at this period (§ 27). l. 4. refers to Constantine. l. 5. **qui** = *cui*. l. 7. **Filippo** (§ 27).

LXXIII. Epitaph in rude Hexameters, from near Nola. 359 A.D. (*C.I.L.* x. 1338.)

semper ob meritum uincis praeconia laudis
et bona progenies quaeret tua fortia facta,
rerum summa coros melius exercendos docet.
belle quidem tua ex ordine gesta naremus;
iam me uincet amor, nequeo tenere dolorem.
laeta quidem semper Felicis nomine ducta,
laetior ut essis iacis in pace fidelis,
abis ut decuit Felicis pace perennem
Eusebio et Ypatio coss. dep(osita) in p(ace) VI kal. Iun.

Notice the acrostic formed by the initial letters of each line, *Serbillae.* l. 2. **fortia facta,** the current Latin phrase for our 'doughty deeds.' Cf. Virg. *Aen.* x. 369:—

> Per vos et fortia facta,
> Per ducis Euandri nomen devictaque bella.

l. 3., i.e. in heaven. l. 4. *naro* is a spelling recommended by various Roman Grammarians (cf. *gnărus*). (See *nárrem*, No. 64.) l. 7. **essis** = *essēs,* **iacis** = *iacēs* (§ 27). l. 8. **abis** = *habēs* (§ 27).

LXXIV. Epitaph in rude Hexameters, from Rome. Fourth century A.D. (*C.I.L.* vi. 30123.)

. . . paucis] mensibus actis
post nuptias, tenero per quam biduatus amore est,
casta cui coiux c[ubilia seruat amorem]
posteris ostendens, ulli si credere fas est.
patre repugnante propio hec nomine signat
nobercam uincens. fame nomen ubiquem.

l. 2. **biduatus**=*viduatus*. l. 3. *cui*. l. 5. The father, at the step-mother's instigation, refused to go to the expense of a tomb. **propio** = *proprio*. The sound of *r* in two successive syllables was unpleasing to the Romans. Hence *increbesco* for *increbresco*, *praestigiae* for *praestrigiae*, etc. (p. 25; *Hist. Gram.* ch. ii. § 18.) **hec** = *haec*. l. 6. **nobercam** = *novercam*, **fame**, etc., for *famae sed nomen ubique* (*est*).

LXXV. Epitaph in rude Hexameters, from Syria. Fourth or fifth century. (*C.I.L.* III. 124).

 sede sub hac recubat clarus praetorique- praefectus
 Maiorinos uirtute caelebratus magna per orbem.
 haec illi nuc requies fati, haec sedis aeterna
 Filippi extructa studiis gratique nepotis.

l. 2. **Maiorinos** = Μαιουρῖνος. **caelebratus** = *celebratus*. l. 3. **nuc** = *nunc*. l. 4. **Filippi** = *Philippi*.

LXXVI. Epitaph of a bishop in rude Hexameters. Algiers. — 440 A.D. (*C.I.L.* VIII. 8634.)

 hic iacet antistes sanctusque Nouatus
 ter denos et VII sedis qui meruit annos.
 precessit die X kal. Septb. (anno) pr(ouinciae) CCCCI.

LXXVII. Epitaph in rude Hexameters, from the district of the Hirpini, 469 A.D. (*Not. Scav.* 1893, p. 422.)

 hic Lucianus cum bona pace quiescit.
 innoces mansuetus mites letus cum amicis amicus
 uixit annis pl(us) m(inus) L nulla manente querella
depositus est in pace die . . kl. Septembres Flabio Marciano et Zenone u(iris) [cl. cons.].

LXXVIII. From a sermon of Avitus, archbishop of Vienne, delivered on the consecration of a church at Annemasse, near Geneva, c. 520 A.D. The sermon is preserved in a papyrus Ms. of the sixth century in the Bibliothèque Nationale, Paris.

Habeat hic caelestis cultur reditus suos, legat hic de lacrimarum riu[lis] manepolos gaudiorum. Exeguetas praesentes tabernaculi reponendi satis est ampla mercidi; quamuis multum orreis sullercia ruralis apponet, spiritalis tamen fecundetas fructus hic congregat . . . quia hodiae Zaccheus noster Abrahae sui filius declaratur, hic christus cum gaudio mansur permansurus excipetur; hic iuxta euangelii regolam pauperebus thesaurus aperitur. Salus quae facta est hodie domicilio crescat et domino sic refectione duplecata germine benedicatur prouentibus ubertatis terra temporaneis, uilla perpetuis; illa pauperis nutriat, haec fidelis; ibi corporum suppetat pastus, hic mentium; quicquid illic largitio sparserit, hic adunet oratio; et quia bene recognuscit hodie condetur meritum suum. Hospis eram et collegistis me; et quicquid fecistis uni ex minimis meis mihi fecistis. Succedat Christus, hospicio introeat; quod adtrahetur, suscipiat; quod offertur, benedicat; quod instetuit, restituat; inuitetur uotis, teneatur factis, caedatur in sacrificiis, pascatur in paruolis.

cultur = *cultor;* manepolos = *manipulos;* praesentes = *praesentis;* mansur = *mansor;* recognuscit = *recognoscit.*

LXXIX. Epitaph of a bishop in rude Hexameters, from Spain. Early part of sixth century. (Rossi, *Inscr. Christ. Rom.* II. 294, 3.)

    te Ioannem Tarraco coluit mirificum uatem
    tuosque in hoc loco in pace condidit artus.

in te libra morum, in te modestia tenuit regnum,
nitens eloquio mitissimus pollebas in corde
gerens curam pauperum, pietate preditus ampla.
sanctus namque uita, fide magnificentius ipse
apparuisti cunctis pergens ad premia Christi.
tuum nempe nomen tuamque dulcissimam mentem
laudabunt posteri, numquam abolenda per euum.
merita praeconiis adtollunt facta per saeclis.
denis equo libram*ine reme*antibus lustris
rector doctorque prefuisti monacis et populis
octiens denos uita peragens feliciter annos.

LXXX. Rude Hexameters from Algiers, 539 A.D. (*C.I.L.* VIII. 5352.)

una et bis senas turres crescebant in ordine totas,
mirabilem operam cito constructa uidetur.
posticius sub termas balteo concluditur ferro.
nullus malorum poterit erigere manum,
patrici Solomonis institutionem nemo expugnare ualeuit.
defensio martirum tuetur posticius ipse,
Clemens et Vincentius martires custodiunt introitum ipsum.

The lines are scanned according to accent and numeration of syllables, but all sense of 'quantity' is lost. Notice the barbarous use of the accusative for the nominative in ll. 1, 2. **posticius** = *porta postica*.

LXXXI. Epitaph in rude Hexameters, from Dalmatia, 599 A.D. (*C.I.L.* III. Suppl. 9527.)

hic iacit Iohannes peccatur et indignus
presbiter. expleto annorum circulo quinto
hunc sibi sepulcrum Iohannis condere iussit

Marcellino suo pro consule nato
germano praesente simul cunctosque nepotes.
ornauit tumolum mente fideli defunctus,
accessit obsis una cum coniuge natis
Anastasii seruans reuerenda limina sancti.
tertio post decimum Augusti numero mensis
ind(ictione) II praefiniuit saeculi diem.

LXXXII. Epitaph of an Abbot, from Spain, 630 A.D. (Hübner *Inscr. Hisp. Christ.* 142.)

haec tenet orna tuum uenerandum corpus Uincenti abbatix
set tua sacra tenet anima caeleste, sacerdos,
regnum, mutasti in melius cum gaudia uite.
martiris exempla signat, cuod membra sacrata
demonstrante deo uatis hic repperit index.
cuater decies cuinos et duos uixerat annos,
misterium Christi mente sincera minister.
raptus aetereas subito sic uenit ad auras,
sic simul officium finis uitamcue remouit,
spiritus adueniens domini cuo tempore sanctus
in regionem piam uixit animamcue locabit.
omnibus his mox est de flammis tollere flammas.
    obiit in p(ace) d. V id. Mart. era DCLXVIII.

l. 1. **abbatix** = *abbātis*. (§ 27.) **orna** = *urna*. l. 4. It is not clear what is referred to. l. 7. **misterium** = *mysteriorum*. l. 11. **uixit** = *uexit;* **locabit** = *locauit*. (§ 27.)

LXXXIII. Attestation of witness to a grant to the Church at Ravenna, probably in the early part of the seventh cent. A.D. The document is in the Library of the Earl of Crawford and Balcarres.

Anastasius uir honestus Excabiss' huic chartule usufructuariae donationis suprascriptarum sex unciarum principalium in integro supernuminate totius supstantie mubile et inmubile sisequae mouentibus, sicut superius legitur, facta in suprascripta sancta. Ravennate ecclesia a Johanne uiro clarissimo expathario, qui dicitur, Georgio magistro militum et nunc primicerius numeri filicum Theudosiacus suprascripto donature, qui mi presente signum sancte crucis ficit et cora nubis ei relicta est, rogatus ab eodem testis suscribsi et de conserbandes omnibus que superius adscripta leguntur ad sancta euangelia corporaliter mei presentia prebuit sacramenta et hanc donatione ab eodem predicto Iohanne acture prenuminate sancte Rauennati aecclesie traditam uidi.

mubile = *mobili*, **sisequae** = *seseque*, **expathario** = *spathario*, like *iscola* (Fr. école) (§ 27), **ficit** = *fecit*, **cora nubis** = *coram nobis*, **conserbandes** = *conservandis*.

LXXXIV. Judgment by Thierry III, King of the French, on a claim, by a woman named Acchildis against Amalgarius, of a portion of land, 679–680 A.D. The document is preserved in the Archives Nationales, Paris.

Theudericus rex Francorum, uir inluster.

Cum ante dies in nostri uel procerum nostrorum presencia conpendio in palacio nostro ibique ueniens fimena nomene Acchildis Amalgario interpellauit, dum dicerit eo quod porcione sua in uilla Noncobanti Bactilione ualle, quem de parti genetrici sua Bertane quondam ligebus obuenire debuerat, post se malo ordene retenirit; qui ipse Amalgarius taliter dedit in respunsis eo quod ipsa terra in predicto loco Bactilione ualle de annus triginta et uno inter ipso Amalgario uel genetore suo Gaeltramno quondam semper tenuerant et possiderant, sic eidem nunc a nostris procerebus ipsius Amalgario fuissit, iudecatum ut de nouo denomenatus aput sex, sua mano septima, dies duos ante istas kalendas Iulias in oraturio nostro super cappella domni Martine, ubi reliqua sacramenta percurribant, hoc dibirit coniurare quod antedicta terra in predicto loco Bactilione ualle inter ipso Amalgario uel genetore suo Gaeltramno de annus triginta et uno semper tenuissint et possedissint, nec eis diger numquam fuissit, nec aliut exinde non redebirit nisi edonio sacramento. Sed ueniens antedictus Amalgarius ad ipso placito Lusareca in palacio nostro uno cum hamedius suos, ipso sacramento iusta quod eidem fuit iudicatum et nostras equalis precepcionis locuntur, in quantum inluster uir Dructoaldus comes palati noster testimuniauit ligibus uisus fuit adimplissit, et tam ipse quam et hamediae suae diliguas eorum derexsissint. Propteria iobimus ut ipsa porcione in predicto loco Bactilione uualle, unde inter eus orta fuit intencio, memoratus Amalgarius contra ipsa Acchilde uel suis heridibus omne tempore abiat euindecata.

    Odinberthus recognouit.

Datum sub die segundo kalendas Iulias annum vii rigni nostri Lusareca in dei nomene f[eliciter].

LXXXV. Rhyming epitaph from the neighbourhood of Corduba. 7th cent. A.D.? (*Inscr. Hisp. Christ.* 132.)

    hic Teudefredi condita
    membra quiescunt arida,
    cujus origo fulgida
    brebe refulsit inclita.

    . . . . .

LXXXVI. Judgment of Pepin, Mayor of the Palace, awarding to Fulradus, Abbot of St. Denis, property in a place called Curbrius, in the province of Telle, against the claim of Ragana, Abbess of Sept Meules. 750 A.D. The document is preserved in the Archives Nationales, Paris.

Cum resedissit inluster uir Pippinus, maiorem domus Attiniaco in palacio publico ad uniuersorum causas audiendum uel recta iudicia termenandum, ibique ueniens Fulradus, abba de monastherio sancti domni Dionisii, ubi ipse preciosus domnus in corpore requiescit, aduocato Ragane abbatissa nomene legitemo interpellabat, repetebat ei eo quod ipsa Ragana uel agentis monasterii sui Septemolas res sancti Dionisii post se malo urdine retenebat iniuste in loco qui dicitur Curbrius in pago Tellau, quem Chairebaldus et coniux sua Aillerta per eorum testamentum ad casa sancti Dionisii condonarunt. Sed ipsi legitemus in presente adistabat et ibidem ostendebat cartas de nomene Francane, qualiter ipsas res ad Septemolas condonassit. Unde et nos acc causa pro ueretate inquesiuimus quod ipsas ris per drictum ad casa sancti Dionisii aderant et ipsi legitemus nulla habuit quod contra ipsa istrumenta sancti Dionisii dicere aut obponere dibuissit. Unde et de presente ipsa strumenta in omnibus ueraces esse dixit, et postea per suo uuadio ipsi Fulrado abbati de ipsas res in Curborio per suo uuadio in causa sancti Dionisii uisus fuit reuestisse, et per suo fistugo sibi exinde dixit esse exitum tam pro se quam pro ipsius Raganam abbatissa uel agentis monastherii sui Septemolas . . . Propteria iobemus ut, dum ac causa sic acta uel perpetrata fuit, ipsi Fulradus alba uel casa sancti Dionisii seo successoris sui ipsas ris in Corborio, de quantum quod Chairebaldus et coniux sua Aillerta per eorum

istrumentum manus potestadiuas ad casa sancti Dionisii condonarunt contra ipsa Ragane abbatissa uel agentis monastherii sui
Septemolas uel in contra ipsius legitemo seo successoris eorum
habiat euindicatas atque elidiatas et sit inter eos in postmodum
ex ac re omneque tempore subita causacio.

   Uuineramnus recognouit et subscripsit.

 Notice **acc** and **ac** for *hac* (§ 27), a spelling which has caused much confusion in Mss. of Latin authors; **drictum** (Fr. droit); **uuadio** with **uu** to express the sound of our *w*, now that Latin *v* (*u*) had passed into the sound of our *v*; **seo** for *seu* (disyll.)

INDEX.

[NUMBERS REFER TO PAGES.]

Ablative Sing. in -*d*, 50, 58.
Accent, 1 *sqq.*, 14 *sq.*, 117 ; Secondary, 15.
Accented Metre, 15, 117.
ad and *at*, 51.
ae and *e*, 115.
Aemilius Paulus, Decree of, 57.
af, 75.
Aleria, 41.
Aletrium Temple Inscr., 83.
alis for *alius*, 93.
Alphabet, earliest Latin, 8.
Ancyranum Monumentum, 103.
Apex, 76.
ar- for *ad-*, 57, 66.
arf(uerunt), 66.
aruorsum, 57.
Arval Hymn (see Carmen Arvale).
asom fero, 31.
atallam, 103.
Atilius Sarranus, inscr. of, 73 *sq.*
Augusti Res Gestae (see Ancyranum).
Aurilius, 38.
Auxiliary Verbs in Late Latin, 116.
Avitus, Sermon of, 125.

b and *v*, 116.
Bacchanalibus, S. C. de, 59 *sqq.*
Bantia, Law of, 80.
boum, 16.
Breves Breviantes, Law of, 48.

c, the letter, 8 ; before *e*, *i*, 116.
C. for *Gaius*, 10.
calecandam, 84.
Capua, inscrr. of magistrates of, 88 *sq.*
Carmen Arvale, 25.
Carmina Saliaria, 26.
cena, 32.
Cerus, 27.
ci and *ti*, 116.
circare (Fr. chercher), 120.
Claudius, inscr. of Emp., 106 *sqq.*
-clum and *-culum*, 55.
Cn. for *Gnaeus*, 10.
Columna Rostrata, 45 *sq.*
Commentarius Ludorum Saecularium (see Lud.).
conquaeisiuei, 76.
contio, 66.
ct and *tt*, 116.

d and *t*, 51.

-*d* in Abl. Sing., 50.
Dacian Wax-tablet, 118.
damnas, 100.
danunt, 70.
Declension, Early Latin, 11 ; Late Latin, 116.
deda, 44.
dedro, 44.
deus, 16.
Diphthongs, history of, 7, 47.
diplŏma, 120.
domus, 96.
Doubling, of consonant, 48 ; of vowel, 48.
Duelonai, 63.
Duenos, 20.
duntaxat, 82.
duonus, 40.
Dvenos Bowl, 19.

e, written for *ei*, 9 ; and *ae*, 115.
ei and *ī*, 47, 75.
enos, 25.

f, earliest form of letter, 8 ; for Gk. φ, 116.
Faliscan Collegium Coquorum, inscr. of, 67.
fefaked, 18.
fifeltares, 93.
Fifth Declension, 92.
fortia facta, 123.
Furfo Decree, 93.

g, the letter, 9 ; before *e, i*, 117.
Genitive Plur. in *-orum*, 40, 94.
Gnaiuod, 42.

gnatus, 52.
graffiti, Pompeian (see Pomp.).

h, initial, lengthens by position, 122 ; loss of, 116.
haud and *hau*, 51.
Herculanean Papyrus, 110 *sq*.
Herculaneus Pagus (see Pagus).
hĭbus, 42.
hic, Adv., 76.
Hinnad, 38.
huc, 69.

IO-stems, Nom. Sing. of (see Nominative).
-i(s) for *-ius*, 37, 93.

jubeo, 65.
Julia Municipalis Lex, 97 *sqq*.
Julius Caesar, 100.

k, the letter, 9.

l for *ll* in *milia*, etc., 75, 95.
Lases, 25.
Law of Breves Breviantes (see Breves) ; of Accentuation (see Accent).
Letters (see Alphabet).
Leucesie, 27.
Lex Repetundarum (see Rep.) ; Rubria (see Rub.) ; Julia Municipalis (see Jul.).
Luceria inscr., 56.
Ludorum Saecularium Commentarius, 101 *sqq*.

-m, final, 32, 51.

Index.

Maurte, 34.
med, 50.
Minerva, 30.
Monumentum Ancyranum (see Anc.).
Mummius, Dedicatory Inscrr. of, 71 *sqq.*

n, dropped before *s, f,* 52.
necesus, 64.
Nemi, inscrr. from, 32, 36, 38.
nequinont, 70.
ni and *ne,* 63.
Nominative Sing. of IO-stems, 37, 93.
Numasioi, 18.

$\breve{o}$ became $\breve{u}$, when unaccented, 16, 35 ; before *ng,* etc., 17.
o and *u* in Late Latin, 115.
Oinumama, 31.
olorom, 46.
oppidum, 84.
Optative, 21, 56.
oquoltod, 65.
-orum, Gen. Plur. (see Gen.).

paastores, 76.
Paenultima Law of Accentuation, 5.
Pagus Herculaneus, Decree of, 89.
Parasitic Vowel, 35, 57.
parisuma, 42.
partim, 33.
Paulus (see Aemilius Paul.).
Picenum, inscr. of, 44 *sq.*
Pisaurum, inscrr. of, 44 *sq.*

polluctum, 70.
Pompeian graffiti, 111 *sqq.*
pono, posui, 75.
Popillius, milestone of, 74.
poplicus, 65.
Praeneste, inscrr. of, 28 *sqq.*
Praenestine fibula, 18.
Preposition written with Noun, 33.
prop(r)io, 124.
Prosepnai, 30.
pth, 103.

q for *qu,* 21.
qu for *cu* (*quu*), 88, 92.
Quantity in Late Latin, 117.
qui, Adv., 77.
quoiei, 77.

r for *d* (see *ar-*) ; for *s* (see Rhotacism).
Repetundarum Lex, 84.
res divina, 54.
Res Gestae Divi Augusti (see Ancyranum).
Rhotacism, 6.
Romance languages, 114.
Rostrata Columna (see Col.).
Rubria Lex, 96.

s and *x,* 116 ; for *ss* in *causa,* etc., 95.
-s final, 51.
Saeturno-, 29.
Salutus, 36.
Saturnian Metre, 15.
Scipio Epitaphs, 39, 76 *sqq.*
sēd, 50.

seignum, 37.
semunis, 26.
Shortening of Final Vowels, 48.
siremps, 83.
souo- for *suo-*, 68.
Spoletium inscr., 53.
sto, 20.
Sulla, inscrr. in honour of, 92 *sq*.
supera, 92.
Syncope, 5, 118.

taxsat, 82.
ted, 50.
Terebonio, 35.
ti and *ci*, 116.
tt and *ct*, 116 ; for *ss*, 57.

u for $\breve{o}$ (see $\breve{o}$) ; and *o* in Late Latin, 115.

-um, Gen. Plur., 40, 94.

v and *b*, 116.
vĕ- for *vŏ-*, 52.
Vertuleii, Dedicatory Tablet of, 69.
vicesma, 33.
Vowel-weakening, 5, 17.
Vulgar Latin, 114 *sqq*.

Weakening of Vowels (see Vowel-weakening).

x and *s*, 116.
xs for *x*, 73.

y, 94.

z, 94.

www.ingramcontent.com/pod-product-compliance
Lightning Source LLC
LaVergne TN
LVHW092049060526
838201LV00047B/1313